UNLEASHING THE BEAST

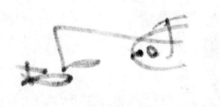

UNLEASHING THE BEAST

HOW A FANATICAL ISLAMIC DICTATOR WILL FORM A TEN-NATION COALITION AND TERRORIZE THE WORLD FOR FORTY-TWO MONTHS

Perry Stone, Jr.

All Scriptures, unless otherwise indicated, are from the *King James Version* of the Bible.

VOICE OF EVANGELISM
TEL: 423.478.3456
FAX: 423.478.1392
WWW.PERRYSTONE.ORG

ISBN: 0-9708611-1-7
Library of Congress Card Number: 2002116175
Copyright ©2003 by Voice of Evangelism, Inc.
P.O. Box 3595
Cleveland, Tennessee 37320
(423) 478-3456
All Rights Reserved
Printed in the United States of America at Pathway Press

DEDICATION

To all of our ministry partners
who assist us in prayer and support,
in our
international outreach ministry

CONTENTS

FOREWORD

Iraq, Osama bin Laden, terroristic threats, weapons of mass destruction, coalitions of nations—what do these things mean to us today?

In the light of Scripture, how do Christians interpret the cataclysmic and apocalyptic incidents of the past few years on the global scene? These events have changed the thinking of people everywhere, and have shaped the future of the world in such a way that even to the world, the events prophesied in the Book of Revelation seem not only possible, but inevitable.

No voice on the horizon today speaks with as much clarity, understanding and Scriptural basis as does the voice of Evangelist Perry F. Stone, Jr. God uses him in ministry on nearly every continent. He preaches and teaches daily by way of his books and magazine, his personal appearances and especially, through the electronic media.

As you read this landmark volume on current events clarified through the lenses of God's prophetic Word, you will grow spiritually and will have a greater appreciation of our conquering Lord Jesus who still controls the trends and movements of history.

An evangelist with an impeccable testimony of God's anointing and power, Perry Stone is indeed God's man for this hour! His writing is as powerful as his preaching. You cannot read this book without a change of mind about many things; and, hopefully, without a change of heart.

Marcus V. Hand
Editor at large, Pathway Press

INTRODUCTION

And the beast which I saw was like unto a leopard, and his feet were as the feet of a bear, and his mouth as the mouth of a lion: and the dragon gave him his power, and his seat, and great authority.

And I saw one of his heads as it were wounded to death; and his deadly wound was healed: and all the world wondered after the beast.

And they worshipped the dragon which gave power unto the beast: and they worshiped the beast, saying, Who is like unto the beast? who is able to make war with him? (Revelation 13:2-4).

Thunder rumbles on the distant horizon. The sky grows darker on the perimeter and the winds are gaining force. The storm is surely coming. The question is not *if* lighting will strike, but *when*. In the distant future an evil kingdom, identified in Scripture as the kingdom of the beast, will rise from the abyss of world darkness. But a smoke will precede the opening of this chasm of destruction, *and it is already appearing*! The thunderous noise of collapsing buildings, the awesome spectacle of steel melting under intense heat, and suffocating clouds of powdery dust give us glimpses into the future of the coming Tribulation.

The September 11, 2001 collapse of the Twin Towers of the World Trade Center, the gaping hole in a section of the Pentagon, and the imprint of an airplane imbedded on the ground in Pennsylvania are events that initiated a conflict which is continuing to build. Years from now, the conflict will climax in a huge valley in Israel, a conflict described in Biblical prophecy and called the Battle of Armageddon (Revelation 16:16).

For 25 years, I have taught the truths of the inspired Scripture, including the amazing accuracy of Biblical prophecy. Teaching what the Bible says about the future has been like going from one mountain to another, with a river below and no bridge to cross. You know where you are and can see where you are going, but you are uncertain of how to link the two mountains and cross the river. Throughout my ministry I have preached from mountain to mountain, declaring the visions and dreams of the Biblical prophets.

Yet, the single event that would bridge the mountains was a mystery. For years, I have looked for that bridge. The pre-planned attack on America by Muslim fanatics, I believe, was the missing piece of the prophetic puzzle. It is the bridge between the mountains. This key sets in motion the last days and the future wars that were revealed to the prophets of the Bible.

How could a terrorist attack have such an impact, and be the trigger on the gun that is pointed toward Israel, America, and other nations? It is critical because this is a religious conflict involving the three monotheistic religions of the world: Christianity, Judaism and Islam. The ancient people of the Book, the Jews, and the Cross of Christianity will clash with the crescent moon, the emblem of Islam.

The coming crisis is often described by sociologists as a clash of cultures. In the eyes of secular America, the Orthodox Jew is a peculiar character. Westerners see images of Jews draped in a white tallith or prayer shawl, dark curls bouncing off their cheeks, and praying in front of a huge wall of rocks at the Western Wall in Jerusalem, and view them as living in a world all their own. Some of the more educated in society view many Muslims as uneducated shepherds, sitting on the ground in goatskin tents, sipping Turkish coffee and telling tall tells originating in Arabia.

Among the Middle Eastern people, America is often viewed as the nation which is spreading the cancer of media violence and sex. These stereotypes paint the three cultures on a canvas of conflict. But the future violence predicted at the hands of the beast of Biblical prophecy does not occur because of cultural differences. The world's final conflict will be a war over the religious beliefs of mankind.

This is not a new struggle. The first bloodshed in the Bible occurred when Cain became jealous of his brother's offering to God (see Genesis 4:2-9). Since that time, the blood of the righteous has soaked the soil of the earth. Christ even warned the Jews that they would be persecuted and killed by those who were deceived, thinking they were doing God's will (John 16:2).

Today, the crescent moon of Islam is rising. According to their beliefs and traditions, the Islamic religion will one day convert the entire world to Islam. Leading this Islamic revival is the *Mahdi*, a coming leader who will assume the role of messiah. Islamic tradition teaches that Jesus will return and follow the Mahdi to Jerusalem, where Jesus will deny that He is the Son of God.

Together, they say, the two will destroy the Cross (Christianity) and kill the Jews who will be hiding behind rocks. Afterwards, Islamic justice will prevail and the world will submit to the rule of the Mahdi and Jesus. It should be noted that the Islamic "Jesus" is actually a Muslim. This apocalyptic belief is being planted in the hearts of over a billion Muslims today. Many of the fanatical groups believe it is their time to make the move against Israel and the West, especially America and Great Britain.

These apocalyptic Muslims believe that weapons of mass destruction, including nuclear, chemical and biological ones, must be used to wipe out the "infidels," or Christians and Jews. Their ideas and expectations clearly match the many predictions the Biblical prophets laid down in the Scripture. From the description of the weapons and the location of the wars, to the eerie comparison of the Mahdi to the Biblical Antichrist who will rule the world for 42 months, his kingdom will be, as I will show, an Islamic empire.

This fanatical regime, united by 10 kings or heads of state, will become the "kingdom of the Beast" that is described in the apocalyptic books of Daniel and Revelation. The book you hold in your hand will document the prophecies and compare the expectations of the Islamic world to the words of the inspired prophets of the Bible.

In the end, three major religions will act out an end-time scenario—a drama whose script was written on parchment long ago by visionaries called prophets. The final battle will be fought over the city of Jerusalem. The day America declared war on terrorism, we blew a crack in the abyss. Soon, the strongest spirit in the kingdom of darkness will be released on earth and the prophecies will be fulfilled.

> The beast that thou sawest was, and is not; and shall ascend out of the bottomless pit (abyss), and go into perdition: and they that dwell on the earth shall wonder, whose names were not written in the book of life from the foundation of the world, when they behold the beast that was, and is not, and yet is (Revelation 17:8).

One

THE BEAST KNOWN
AS THE ANTICHRIST

And I stood upon the sand of the sea, and saw a beast rise up out of the sea, having seven heads and ten horns, and upon his horns ten crowns, and upon his heads the name of blasphemy. And the beast which I saw was like unto a leopard, and his feet were as the feet of a bear, and his mouth as the mouth of a lion: and the dragon gave him his power, and his seat, and great authority. And I saw one of his heads as it were wounded to death; and his deadly wound was healed: and all the world wondered after the beast (Revelation 13:1-3).

Few Christians living today have never heard the term *antichrist*. The average Christian in the Western hemisphere who has read prophecy books, watched prophetic videos or viewed Christian television programs understands four basic facts revealed in Scripture about the future Antichrist.

- The Antichrist is a man who will rule a global empire at the end of the age.
- He will make a treaty of peace for seven years.
- He will eventually set up his kingdom in Jerusalem.
- He will help instigate the final battle called Armageddon.

Daniel, the Biblical prophet, and the Apostle John both used abundant space in their writings, giving readers amazing details concerning this man's rise to power, his realm of influence, and his reaction to those who reject his mission. Much of our present understanding of this man and his kingdom comes from these two prophetic books.

After studying this subject for 25 years, I have discovered that there are many facts in the Bible which allude to this person. I also realize that some teaching is based on tradition or private interpretation handed down from generation to generation and may have little Biblical or historical foundation.

For example, you may have attended a prophetic conference or read research material that taught the following: The Antichrist will be a Jew from the tribe of Dan; he will rebuild a Temple for the Jews on the Temple Mount in Jerusalem; and he will be a man of peace and will be the head of the European Union.

These three theories are based on individual interpretations or denominational traditions, and not entirely upon the Scriptures themselves. In fact, I will show that there is much more information referencing the Antichrist that has not been taught, than has been released in recent years. After 25 years of ministry and over 30,000 hours of Biblical study and research, I believe, and I will explain to you, the following:

- The Antichrist will be a Gentile (of Islamic back-ground) and not a Jew.
- He will not rebuild the Jewish Temple; the prophet Elijah will.
- He will control more than just the Common Market.

♦ He will bring peace only to his followers, and death to those who resist.

THE ANTICHRIST: A GENTILE, NOT A JEW

During the second and third centuries, there was much animosity between Christian leaders and Jewish rabbis. Many of the early church fathers became very anti-Semitic in their theology. Some taught that the Antichrist would be a Jew from the tribe of Dan, which they based upon Jacob's prophecy about Dan in Genesis:

> Dan shall be a serpent by the way, an adder in the path, that biteth the horse heels, so that his rider shall fall backward (Genesis 49:17).

Early in the third century, Hippolytus, an early church father who is called by some "the most important theologian in the pre-Constantinian era," quoted the prophecy Moses spoke over the tribe of Dan: "And of Dan he said, Dan is a lion's whelp: he shall leap from Bashan" (Deuteronomy 33:22). Hippolytus wrote in *Treatise on Christ and Antichrist*::

> Dan is a lion's whelp and, in naming the tribe of Dan, he declared clearly the name of the tribe from which the Antichrist is destined to spring. For as Christ sprang from the tribe of Judah, so the Antichrist is to spring from the tribe of Dan.

The fact that Dan is missing from the tribal listing in Revelation 7:1-8 only adds to the speculation that the future Antichrist must be from that tribe. It must be noted that in early history, the tribe of Dan settled in the area of Bashan, which is the Golan Heights today. Later the tribe of Dan settled near the coast, in the area that is today Tel-Aviv. The Tel-Aviv area has a strong population of secular, agnostic, and atheistic Jews. This may be why the region of Dan is omitted from Revelation 7. Others speculate that if the Antichrist were "opposite of

Christ," he must be a Jew because Christ was of Jewish origin. He must arise from inside of Israel, they reason, since Christ was born in Israel (Luke 2:11). Further, he must be from a tribe since Christ was identified with a tribe—namely Judah (Micah 5:2).

Some have gone so far as to say the Antichrist will claim he was born of a virgin, since Christ was born of the virgin (Matthew 1:23). Let me point out that the word *antichrist* does not mean "one like Christ," but "one instead of, or against, Christ." The Antichrist will actually be against Christ and make no claims to be Christ himself. Still, the future false prophet in Revelation 18:11 may attempt to deceive the world into believing that he is Christ.

Over the years I have heard men teach that the Antichrist would be a Jewish leader from Israel. I was puzzled, however, knowing that the world's 1.2 billion Muslims would never accept a Jew from Israel to rule or control the Muslim nations.

After many trips to Israel, I began asking noted prophetic teachers why nobody was teaching about the role Muslims will play in prophecy. Prophetic teachers consistently spoke about Israel and the Jews, along with the Gentile dominated Common Market, now the European Union. But for years, writers and researchers of prophecy have seemed to ignore the importance of the Islamic religion in the future affairs of the Middle East and Europe.

In the early 1990's, I met a young girl from Iran who shared with me detailed prophetic beliefs of Iranian Shiite Muslims that few Americans, including myself, had ever heard. After comparing her information with the prophecies of the Bible, I became convinced that the coming Antichrist will be a fanatical Muslim who will proclaim himself to be Islam's final prophet.

A master of war, he will use weapons of mass destruction in order to hold entire nations hostage (see Revelation 13:4).

Those who do not convert to his religion will be beheaded and others forced into starvation (see Revelation 13:15-17 and 20:4). Before thinking this is mere prophetic fiction, take a journey with me into the Scriptures for a clearer picture of the Antichrist of Biblical prophecy.

THE WORD *ANTICHRIST* IN SCRIPTURE

The word *antichrist* was coined by the Apostle John, who authored St. John's Gospel, I, II and III John, and the Book of Revelation. The word *antichrist* is found only in John's Epistles. It can mean "against Christ" or "instead of Christ."

W.E. Vines' Greek dictionary comments on this word: "By combining the two words *anti* and *Christ*, it can mean *one who assumes the guise of Christ, or opposes Christ.*" Thus the Antichrist is one who is against Christ.

In approximately 90 A.D., John wrote the Epistles of 1, 2 and 3 John. He used the word *antichrist* in four passages:

> Little children, it is the last time: and as ye have heard that antichrist shall come, even now are there many antichrist; whereby we know that it is the last time (1 John 2:18).

> Who is a liar but he that denieth that Jesus is the Christ? He is antichrist, that denieth the Father and the son (v. 22).

> And every spirit that confesseth not that Jesus Christ is come in the flesh is not of God: and this is the spirit of antichrist, whereof ye have heard that it should come; and even now is it in the world (4:3).

> For many deceivers are entered into the world, who confess not that Jesus Christ is come in the flesh. This is a deceiver and an antichrist (2 John 1:7).

Because John said, "Even now there are many antichrists"(1 John 2:18), some teach there is *not* a future person called the Antichrist. They say that the antichrist is only a spirit which has existed from the first church to the present age. I submit to you that antichrist is both a spirit and a future person!

The "antichrist spirit" existed in the time of the early church, because some denied the divinity of Christ and His position as the Son of God. Yet, the Bible says that at the end of days, one man will appear who will be a prince of darkness, a son of perdition, who is identified as the Antichrist. In 2 John 1:7, the Greek uses the definite article, *ho antichristos* meaning "the antichrist."

According to John, the spirit of antichrist and the Antichrist deny three things:

1. Both deny, without hesitation, the deity of Jesus Christ (1 John 2:22).

2. Both deny that Jesus Christ is the Son of God (1 John 2:22).

3. Both deny the relationship between the Father and the Son (1 John 2:22).

Just as the future land of conflict will be Israel and the future city of conflict Jerusalem, so the future spiritual conflict will arise over the person of Jesus Christ. Was He just a man? Was He merely a prophet? Or was He the Son of God?

To the religious Jew, Jesus Christ was simply a man of history who formed a new religion. To the Muslims, Jesus Christ was one of the prophets of Allah. But to the true Christian, Jesus Christ is the Son of the Living God (see Matthew 14:33, 27:53, Romans 1:4).

Further evidence that the Antichrist is a mortal man and not just an evil spirit can be viewed in light of other New Testament passages that make use of personal pronouns. Evangelical scholars point to the following passages that reveal important details about this future world dictator. In each case, he is identified with the use of a masculine pronoun:

♦ The Antichrist is called "the man of sin," "the son of perdition" (2 Thessalonians 2:3).

- "He as God sitteth in the temple of God, showing himself that he is God" (v. 4).
- He will "be revealed in his time" (v. 6).
- The dragon gave him his power, and his seat, and great authority (Revelation 13:2).
- Who is able to make war with him? And there was given unto him a mouth speaking great things and blasphemies; and power was given unto him to continue forty and two months (vv. 4, 5).
- It was given unto him to make war (v. 7).

Even in John's writings, the beloved disciple distinguished the *spirit* of antichrist from the *person* of Antichrist. In 1 John 2:22, the Greek Interlinear reads, "Who is the liar if it is not the one that denies that Jesus is Christ? This is the Antichrist."

The phrase "the antichrist" is *ho antichristos* and alludes to a specific person. The spirit of antichrist was working in John's day as heretics were writing against Christ's deity, but the Antichrist, the man of end-time prophecy, is yet to come.

NAMES GIVEN TO THE ANTICHRIST

Bible scholars for centuries have identified many other passages that speak of this final world leader. The Scripture gives a list of names that help us to further identify this man. The names are descriptive words; they identify the character and the nature of this man who will be the Antichrist.

1. The little horn, *Daniel 7:8*
2. King of fierce countenance, *8:23*
3. The prince that shall come, *9:26*
4. The desolate storm, *v. 27*
5. The willful king, *11:36*
6. The man of sin, *2 Thessalonians 2:3*

7. The son of perdition, *v. 3*

8. The Antichrist, *1 John 2:22*

9. The Beast, *Revelation 11:7*

WRITINGS FROM THE EARLY CHURCH

The early church fathers were bishops and leaders who lived and wrote from the first to the fourth centuries. They made numerous statements concerning the rise of the Antichrist. At one point in the first century, some felt that the wicked Roman Emperor, Nero, had faked his death and would rise once again from the East.

> He (the antichrist) shall divide the globe into three ruling powers when, moreover, Nero shall be raised up from hell. Elias shall first come to seal the beloved one; at which things the region of Africa and the northern nation, the whole earth from all sides, for seven years shall tremble.
>
> But Elias shall occupy the half of the time and Nero shall occupy half *(Ante-Nicene Fathers,* Volume IV, Chapter XLI).

Nero was such a persecutor of Christians that when he died some believed he would come back from the dead in the form of the Antichrist. The writer used the verse in Revelation concerning the beast that "was and is not shall come out of the pit," and applied this to Nero (see Revelation 17:11). This is an incorrect interpretation of Scripture and tradition.

Because both Judas and the Antichrist are called "the son of perdition" in the Bible (John 17:12; 2 Thessalonians 2:3), some commentators believe that Judas will once again come back from hell in the form of the Antichrist. The thought that since Judas "went to his own place" at his death (Acts 1:25), he is being preserved and will later arise as the Antichrist.

This idea is against both logic and sound Scriptural interpretation. The fact is, there is a spirit that will come from the underground abyss and take possession of the

Antichrist, but no departed man will come forth from hell and be reincarnated as this future deceiver. However, a powerful evil spirit now confined under the earth in a chamber called the abyss will be released in the future. This spirit will possess the Antichrist, giving him great power over the world.

> The beast that thou sawest was, and is not; and shall ascend out of the bottomless pit, and go into perdition: and they that dwell on the earth shall wonder, whose names were not written in the book of life from the foundation of the world, when they behold the beast that was, and is not, and yet is (Revelation 17:8).

Other statements are made about the Antichrist in early church writings:

> When the close of time draws near, a great prophet shall be sent from God to turn men to the knowledge of God, and he shall receive power of doing wonderful things. . . . And when his work shall be accomplished, another king shall arise out of Syria, born from an evil spirit, the over thrower and destroyer of the human race, who shall destroy that which is left by the former evil, together with himself.
>
> . . . .
>
> Now this is he who is called Antichrist; but he shall falsely call himself Christ, and shall fight against the truth, and being overcome shall flee; and shall renew the war, and often be conquered, until in the fourth battle, all the wicked shall be slain, subdued and captured, he shall at length pay the penalty of his crimes. . . . (Ante-Nicene Fathers, Book VII, Chapter XVIII.)

In a section called "Fragments From The Commentaries," referring to Daniel, we read;

> And I inquired about the fourth beast. It is the fourth kingdom of which we have already spoken, that he refers: the kingdom, than which no greater kingdom of like nature has

arisen upon the earth; from which also ten horns are to spring, and to be apportioned among ten crowns.

And amid these another little horn shall rise, which is that of Antichrist. And it shall pluck by the roots the three others before it; that is to say, he shall subvert the three kings of Egypt, Lybia, and Ethiopia, with the view of acquiring for himself universal domain.

And after conquering the remaining seven horns, he will at last being inflated by a strange and wicked spirit, to stir up war against the saints, and to persecute all everywhere, with the aim of being glorified by all, and being worshiped as God.

There are many more church traditions concerning the Antichrist. Bishop Hippolytus said: "In the same manner also will the accuser come forth from an impure woman upon the earth, but shall be born of a virgin spuriously." These early traditions are interesting, and shed light on the subject.

Yet, the Bible gives ample revelation and understanding concerning the Antichrist and his kingdom. The future Antichrist and his final kingdom are an important theme in the latter writings of the New Testament and in the thinking and records of the early church and early fathers. Biblical research indicates the Antichrist will form a final earthly kingdom cemented together with the support of 10 other world leaders, and will dominate the world scene for 42 months.

This will be the kingdom of the Beast.

Two

THE KINGDOM OF THE BEAST

After this I saw in the night visions, and behold a fourth beast, dreadful and terrible, and strong exceedingly; and it had great iron teeth: it devoured and brake in pieces, and stamped the residue with the feet of it: and it was diverse from all the beasts that were before it; and it had ten horns.

I considered the horns, and, behold, there came up among them another little horn, before whom there were three of the first horns plucked up by the roots: and, behold, in this horn were eyes like the eyes of man, and a mouth speaking great things (Daniel 7:7, 8).

Both Daniel and the apostle John were visionaries who saw the future. Inspired by the Holy Spirit, they pierced the veil to reveal future empires that would one day dominate the world and impact the nation of Israel. Both men used descriptive language and characterized the kingdoms they saw as beasts that would arise. In Daniel 7:2, 3, the prophet saw four great beasts rising out of the sea.

The first was a ferocious lion. He was followed by a roving bear, who in turn was followed by a cunning leopard. The fourth beast was so different from the previous three that it is often called a non-descriptive beast. This final beast was a mysterious creature with seven heads and ten horns. Daniel was told that these four great beasts were four kingdoms that would arise from the earth (Daniel 7:17, 23).

History itself has interpreted the meaning. The lion was ancient Babylon. The bear represented the Medes and Persians that overthrew the Babylonians in Babylon. After the Medes and Persians, the Grecians, under the leadership of Alexander the Great, swallowed up all the previous empires and added other kingdoms and regions to its tally of nations. The fourth empire in the succession was the Roman Empire. This was the empire that ruled in the time of Christ and the first century apostles. Thus the four major empires in Daniel's ancient prophecy were:

1. The Babylonian Empire

2. The Medio-Persian Empire

3. The Grecian Empire

4. The Roman Empire

Some common elements link these empires of history and prophecy:

♦ All four empires ruled the Mediterranean Sea area.

♦ All four empires invaded and controlled Egypt.

♦ All four empires were involved in dealing with Israel and the Jews.

♦ All four empires were involved in dealing with Jerusalem and the Temple.

♦ All four empires were Gentile empires with Gentile rulers.

♦ Three of the four empires ruled from the area of Babylon.

Traditionally, prophetic scholars point out that the fourth beast represents the Roman Empire. Certainly this is correct. Yet, out of the same territory of the ancient Roman Empire will emerge a final kingdom of prophecy, including 10 horns that represent 10 kings ruling over 10 kingdoms. These 10 kings and kingdoms will form and unite at the time of the end:

> After this I saw in the night visions, and behold a fourth beast, dreadful and terrible, and strong exceedingly; and it had great iron teeth: it devoured and brake in pieces, and stamped the residue with the feet of it: and it was diverse from all the beasts that were before it; and it had ten horns (Daniel 7:7).

> And the ten horns out of this kingdom are ten kings that shall arise: and another shall rise after them; and he shall be diverse from the first, and he shall subdue three kings (Daniel 7:24).

The order and succession of these prophetic kingdoms was also revealed to the ancient king of Babylon, King Nebuchadnezzar.

A KING'S NIGHTMARE

In Daniel's time, King Nebuchadnezzar experienced a troubling dream of an image of a man with a head of gold. He had a chest and arms of silver, thighs of brass and legs of iron. Daniel interpreted his dream, telling the king it was a picture of world empires from ancient Babylon until the time that the Lord would set up His kingdom (Daniel 2:31-44). History can now interpret the progression and ruling order of those kingdoms as Babylon, Medio Persia, Greece and Rome.

In the king's dream, the legs of iron on the image (Rome) represented a split that would occur in the Roman kingdom sometime in the future. Historically, this happened when the Roman Empire divided between the East and the West; with Rome, Italy, being the western leg and Constantinople, Turkey (Istanbul today), being the eastern leg.

According to the Book of Daniel, the legs of iron (the division of Rome) will eventually produce 10 toes—which are the same kings and kingdoms identified by both Daniel and John as the 10 horns (Daniel 7:24; Revelation 17:12, 16).

Many prophetic teachers and observers have concluded that the formation of the European Union is the continuation of the old Roman Empire. They see it as the iron legs that eventually will form the 10 toes. For years, men have taught that the EU would have 10 strong nations and, from among those nations, the final world dictator would arise.

Since the EU is a European entity, modern prophecy teachers have assumed the Antichrist will be elected the head of the EU. Some had to change their teaching when the EU expanded its member nation from 10 to 15. An often-overlooked point of this interpretation is that many of the nations that once formed the ancient Roman Empire are not pro-Western nations, but are now Islamic nations. They include:

- Egypt
- Ethiopia
- Libya
- Morocco
- Jordan
- Lebanon
- Northern Iraq
- Syria
- Turkey

Only Italy and Greece, predominantly Catholic and Greek Orthodox, are not on the Islamic list. I contend that Western theologians place too much emphasis on Western Europe and the EU, and not enough on the fact that these Islamic nations make up part of the old Roman territory. They neglect to note that Islam wants to rule the entire Mediterranean and extend the Islamic crescent into all of Europe.

The Muslims' goal is not just to build mosques, but to eventually convert the people in these countries to the religion of Islam. When we examine the geographical regions of the past prophetic empires and the region where the antichrist will rule, we see that Islam controls these nations, with the exception of Greece, Italy and Israel.

The prophet Daniel predicted that when the Antichrist comes to power, he will subdue three kings (Daniel 7:24). Hippolytus and other early church fathers saw these three kings are Egypt, Libya and Ethiopia:

> In those times, then he shall arise and meet them. And when he has overmastered three horns out of the ten in the array of war, and has rooted out, vis., Egypt, Libya, and Ethiopia, and has got their spoil and trappings. . . he will begin to be lifted up in heart, to exalt himself against God as master of the whole world (Hippolytus, *Treatise on Christ and Antichrist*).

Apparently, Hippolytus was referring to Daniel's prophecies that the Antichrist would uproot three kings in Northern Africa. Daniel speaks of three nations the Antichrist will invade and control:

> But he shall have power over the treasures of gold and of silver, and over all the precious things of Egypt: and the Libyans and the Ethiopians shall be at his steps (Daniel 11:43).

Modern teachers emphasize that the countries of the final 10 kings will comprise the European Union (EU) nations, but this cannot be totally accurate. In Nebuchadnezzar's dream, five kings are from the Eastern branch (leg) and five from the Western branch (leg). Most of the current EU nations are Western powers; yet, Egypt, Libya and Ethiopia are not in the EU, but are listed as three of the 10 final kings of Biblical prophecy.

In the past, these three Islamic nations were pro-Western, and Ethiopia was a strong Christian nation. Presently, all three nations have a strong radical Islamic element that is attempting to turn their nation against Israel and the West.

As we will point out, the real key to understanding Biblical teaching relating to the kingdom of the Beast is to understand how Islamic radicals are corrupting certain Islamic teachings for their own benefit. Some have the deliberate and stated purpose of producing a new nation of terrorists and fundamentalists.

Let me point out that the majority of Muslims are not radical or fanatical in their beliefs. I have several Muslim friends in the Middle East whom I believe would protect and defend me if necessary. They introduce me to their friends as a "holy man." But this Beast system of which I speak will unite a radical element that seeks the conquest of those who disagree with their policies. Their most powerful tools will be weapons of mass destruction.

In Revelation, John describes the same beast Daniel saw in his vision 600 years prior:

> And I stood upon the sand of the sea, and saw a beast rise up out of the sea, having seven heads and ten horns, and upon his horns ten crowns, and upon his heads the name of blasphemy. And the beast which I saw was like unto a leopard, and his feet were as the feet of a bear, and his mouth as the mouth of a lion: and the dragon gave him his power, and his seat, and great authority (Revelation 13:1, 2).

Both Daniel and John saw the same beast rising up out of the sea (Daniel 7:3 and Revelation 13:1). Daniel called this sea the Great Sea. Today it is the Mediterranean, the area of the ancient Roman Empire. Both Daniel and John indicate the beast had 10 horns. In Biblical prophecy, horns represent a king or a kingdom. The 10 horns are not the Beast; they are a part of the Beast, just as the horns of a ram are not the ram but a part of the ram.

The Beast itself is some type of kingdom that hosts the 10 horns. The New Testament was written in Greek. John identified the Beast with the word *therion,* meaning "a wild beast." This future beast kingdom is uncontrollable; nations will be unable to tame it. This certainly fits the description of radical Islamic terrorists: they cannot be controlled and they refuse to negotiate.

Many Muslims of Arab descent trace their lineage back to Abraham through Ishmael, Abraham's first son. Ishmael's mother, Hagar, was Sarah's Egyptian servant (see Genesis 16:4-11). Abraham's second son, Isaac, was the son God promised through Sarah, Abraham's wife (Genesis 17:19-21). In fact, some Muslims believe that when Abraham offered Isaac before God (see Genesis 22), it was actually Ishmael who was the chosen son. They believe that the Jews and Christians changed the story and replaced Ishmael with Isaac as the son of promise.

By accepting this distortion, Muslims believe that the land of Israel actually belongs to them and not to the Jews. The fact that many trace their genealogy back to Ishmael brings out this interesting point. God spoke to Hagar, Ishmael's mother, about her son:

> And the angel of the Lord said unto her, Behold, thou art with child, and shalt bear a son, and shalt call his name Ishmael; because the Lord hath heard thy affliction. And he will be a wild man; his hand will be against every man, and every man's hand against him; and he shall dwell in the presence of all his brethren (Genesis 16:11, 12).

Ishmael and his descendants would dwell among the Hebrew people and Ishmael would be a "wild man." The same Hebrew word *wild* is used in the Old Testament 10 times when referring to wild donkeys (see Job 39:5). Ishmael's hand "being against every man" indicates he would be a person who would fight and generate much contention and strife. It also means "having a war-like nature."

Fanatical Muslims in Israel gain global attention through suicide bombings. In the Sudan, Islamic radicals have murdered hundreds of thousands of Christians with little opposition. In America, we know that Islamic terrorists flew planes into the World Trade Center and the Pentegon, killing nearly 3,000 innocent people. In other nations, Christian churches are burned to the ground, children are kidnapped and Christian women are taken as slaves by these religious fanatics.

Secular, moderate Muslims often point out to us that these individuals do not represent the mainstream of Islam. Yet, the number of Muslims who use the name of Allah to bring destruction to non-Muslims seems to be increasing globally. Certainly, to identify this types of fanatic as "wild" is certainly accurate.

THE DANGEROUS BEAST

John used the Greek word meaning *therion,* alluding to a dangerous and wild animal, to describe the final world empire hosted by the Antichrist. Notice that it is not just the Antichrist himself who is dangerous, but the entire Beast kingdom. This includes the 10 horns, or 10 kings, that are a part of this fierce kingdom of darkness.

> And the ten horns which thou sawest are ten kings, which have received no kingdom as yet; but receive power as kings one hour with the beast. These have one mind, and shall give their power and strength unto the beast (Revelation 17:12, 13).

Interestingly, in Daniel 7:24, the Antichrist arises after the 10 kings come to power. In Revelation 17:12, these same 10 kings receive authority in one hour—after they give their kingdoms to the Antichrist:

> The ten horns which thou sawest are ten kings, which have received no kingdom as yet; but receive power as kings one hour with the beast (Revelation 17:12).

In the Book of Daniel, these 10 nations are formed first. Afterward, the Antichrist arises from among them and uproots three nations: Egypt, Libya and Ethiopia. Although these three nations out of the 10 are overthrown, it appears the Antichrist will place his men in leadership positions; thus, 10 nations will still remain a part of his coalition.

According to John, these 10 kings give their authority over to the beast in an hour's time. In return, the Antichrist gives them the benefit of not being overthrown by his armies, but allows them to rule alongside him.

THE SEVEN HEADS OF THE BEAST

In Revelation, the apostle John further reveals that this beast has seven heads. Since apocalyptic writing is often veiled in symbolism, one must examine the Scripture to discover the meaning of these heads.

> And there appeared another wonder in heaven; and behold a great red dragon, having seven heads and ten horns, and seven crowns upon his heads (Revelation 12:3).

> And I stood upon the sand of the sea, and saw a beast rise up out of the sea, having seven heads and ten horns, and upon his horns ten crowns, and upon his heads the name of blasphemy (Revelation 13:1)

> So he carried me away in the spirit into the wilderness: and I saw a woman sit upon a scarlet colored beast, full of names of blasphemy, having seven heads and ten horns (Revelation 17:3).

Who are these seven heads? Why are there seven? For centuries, Bible scholars have noted that these heads represent the major empires that have ruled since the beginning of Biblical history and have effected Israel and the Jews. They are:

1. The Egyptian Empire
2. The Assyrian Empire
3. The Babylonian Empire
4. The Media-Persian Empire

5. The Grecian Empire

6. The Roman Empire

7. The final global empire

When John describes this vision of the beast with seven heads, he informs the reader that the sixth head (kingdom) was in existence and ruling over the world in his day. This would be the Roman Empire. John then explains how a seventh empire will form in the future and "continue for a short space." This seventh empire is often identified as the uniting of Europe, and especially the European Union.

What was revealed to John but was not known to the Old Testament prophets was that out of the previous empires would come an eighth empire, the kingdom of the Beast. This would thrust the world into the worst time of tribulation in world history. Thankfully, the empire will rule for only 42 months.

> And the angel said unto me, Wherefore didst thou marvel? I will tell thee the mystery of the woman, and of the beast that carrieth her, which hath the seven heads and ten horns. The beast that thou sawest was, and is not; and shall ascend out of the bottomless pit, and go into perdition: and they that dwell on the earth shall wonder, whose names were not written in the book of life from the foundation of the world, when they behold the beast that was, and is not, and yet is.
>
> And the beast that was, and is not, even he is the eighth, and is of the seven, and goeth into perdition (Revelation 17:7, 8, 11).

According to John, the final beast arising from the sea (Revelation 13:1) will form an eighth and final empire. Prophetically, the sixth empire of history was Rome. The seventh is a continuation of Rome, involving the EU and the United Nations. But this eighth and concluding empire, as we will show, appears to be an Islamic empire that will swallow up the territory where history's past empires have ruled.

This is why the Beast is a combination of the lion (Babylon), the bear (Media-Persia), and a leopard (Greece) as stated in Revelation 13:2. The kingdom of the Antichrist will have the strength of Babylon, the strict laws of Media-Persia, and the speed to rapidly swallow up opposing nations, as did the Grecians. The Beast kingdom will include the areas where these empires of prophecy have ruled. It will include, but not be limited to, the Middle East, Northern Africa and much of Europe.

Another important point is Revelation 17 where John indicated the future Beast kingdom "was", that is, it *was* a kingdom that had previously existed; it "is not," that is, it *was not in existence in John's day*; and it "shall ascend," meaning *arise in the future*. Is there an empire of Biblical history and prophecy that once existed but no longer existed in John's day (95 A.D.), yet could come alive again in the future?

Of the six empires that ruled from Egypt to the time of Rome, only one is no longer in existence. Egypt is presently the country of Egypt. Greece is a modern nation today, carrying the same ancient name. Syria is the ancient nation known as Assyria.

The Persians are the native people living in Iran who still call themselves Persians (Iran was a name given by the British). Rome is currently the capital of Italy and influences much of Europe through the Roman Catholic Church.

The Babylonian Empire was located in the region now known as Iraq. This ancient empire is presently non-existent, but it is the region of the world where the future Antichrist will arise and rebuild the ancient territory of Babylon. The demonic spirit of ancient Babylon will be unleashed in full measure during the time known as the Tribulation.

This spirit is identified as the "beast that arises out of the abyss" in Revelation 17:8. According to Scripture, these strong wicked spirits have been restrained by God and will, in the future, be unleashed from caverns deep within the earth (Revelation 9:14-15).

When the beast from the pit is released and begins to control the "son of perdition" (the Antichrist), the hot spot will be the territory where ancient Babylon once dominated the world. This will include the modern nations of Iraq, Syria and Lebanon.

THE MYSTERIOUS 10/40 WINDOW

One of the strange spiritual aspects of the ancient Babylonian Empire relates to what is called the "10/40 window." This window is an invisible belt that stretches from West Africa to East Asia, between 10 degrees and 40 degrees north of the equator. The very center of this 10/40 window is in the area of Baghdad, Iraq, which is within 30 miles of the ruins of ancient Babylon!

Many Biblical and historical events occurred in the heart of this 10/40 window. The famous Tower of Babel was built in this area, in the plains of Shinar (Genesis 11:2). It is the region where King Nebuchadnezzar, of Daniel's writings, built Babylon and ruled the world. It is where the Medes and Persians conquered, and the kings of the Medes and Persians seized world power.

Further, ancient Babylon is where Alexander the Great set up his command center. It is where he died drunk at age 33. All of the world's major religions were birthed in the area of this 10/40 window. According to Luis Bush, there are three major religions in this 10/40 block. Muslims number 706 million; Hindus, 800 million; and Buddhists, 300 million. In fact, 95 percent of the world's people who have never heard the Gospel live in the 10/40 window!

The 10/40 window, with Iraq in the very center, is the heart of the Islamic religion and influence! Let's look at these revealing facts:

- The 10/40 window contains a third of the world's land area; yet, two-thirds of the world's population live there.
- Ninety-nine percent of the world's Muslim population lives there.
- The harshest persecution against Christianity today occurs in the 10/40 window.

From a spiritual perspective, this area has historically been controlled by some of the strongest spirits in the realm of darkness. Scholars such as Alexander Hislop, in his book *The Two Babylons*, trace the beginning of all false religions to the Tower of Babel (Genesis 11).

The area of ancient Babylon is the cradle of all counterfeit religions that spread like a plague after the fall of the Tower of Babel. It is also where Daniel encountered a dark prince, the prince of Persia who, for three weeks, hindered the answers to the prophet's prayers (Daniel 10:13).

The nations of the 10/40 window—especially Iran, Iraq and Syria—are, without a doubt, the greatest spiritual strongholds on earth. Most of the opposition against Israel and the Jews has been unleashed from the Persians, the Iraqis and the Syrians. Much of the money used to finance global terrorism can be traced back to their Islamic leaders.

It is clear that our adversary, the Enemy, is holding spiritual chains, like a hangman's noose, around the minds of the people in these Islamic countries. In the next chapter, I will tell you more about how this Enemy will work through the man the Bible calls a Beast!

Three

IDENTIFYING
THE BEAST

After this I saw in the night visions, and behold a fourth beast, dreadful and terrible, and strong exceedingly; and it had great iron teeth: it devoured and brake in pieces, and stamped the residue with the feet of it: and it was diverse from all the beasts that were before it; and it had ten horns.

I considered the horns, and, behold, there came up among them another little horn, before whom there were three of the first horns plucked up by the roots: and, behold, in this horn were eyes like the eyes of man, and a mouth speaking great things. (Daniel 7:7, 8).

The Bible gives us an enormous amount of information relating to the time of the end. Most major Biblical prophets foresaw events pertaining to the last days, and many recorded key bits of information that, when linked with other prophecies, paint a clear picture of the Antichrist and his mission of global dominion. In Scripture, we see that:

- the Antichrist will be a Gentile, not a Jew;
- the Antichrist will arise out of the Middle East; and
- the Antichrist will rule from a small nation before he takes over Jerusalem.

Let us examine these three statements in light of Biblical predictions.

THE ANTICHRIST WILL BE A GENTILE

The fact that the Antichrist will be a Gentile and not a Jew is seen in Biblical typology, imagery, and understanding of the "times of the Gentiles." The Bible makes it clear that, at the time of the end, Gentiles will once again control Israel and Jerusalem for a final 42 months (see Luke 21:24, Revelation 11:1, 2). Once again we refer back to the dream of Nebuchadnezzar.

The king saw an image with a head of gold, a chest and arms of silver, thighs of brass, legs of iron, and feet and toes of iron and clay (Daniel 2: 36-45). This metallic image was a revelation of the future empires that would rule the world from the time of Babylon to the coming of the Lord. Babylon was the head of gold; Media-Persia, the chest and arms of silver; Greece, the thighs of brass; and Rome was symbolized by legs of iron. The Roman Empire eventually split between the East and the West (Rome and Turkey).

In the time of the end, the 10 toes on the image spoke of 10 kings who would rule with one leader, the Antichrist. Antichrist would swallow up three of the kings (Daniel 7:8), and place his own kings in power for the final 42 months of the Tribulation (Revelation 17:12). The main feature of all previous kingdoms of Biblical prophecy is that they were all Gentile powers!

Jesus made it clear that Jerusalem would be trodden down of the Gentiles (Luke 21:24). Christ also revealed this to John in Revelation 11:1, 2. John was told to measure the Tribulation temple in Jerusalem. The instructions were to omit the outer court, "For it is given to the Gentiles and the holy city shall they tread under foot forty and two months" (Revelation 11:2).

The Antichrist and his armies will capture and control Jerusalem for the last 42 months of the 7-year Tribulation. The future Antichrist will form the eighth and final Gentile kingdom prior to the visible return of Christ to earth. Some ask, "But won't the Jews accept him as Messiah?"

The assumption this question reveals is based on two scriptures. *One*, Daniel said, "He will not regard the God of his fathers" (Daniel 11:37). "God of his fathers" refers to the God of Abraham, Isaac and Jacob.

Two, the Bible says in John 5:43 that Jesus came in the Father's name and they wouldn't receive Him, but another would come in his own name and they would receive him. Since the real Jewish Messiah, Christ, came and was not received, it is assumed that a false Jewish messiah will come and be received.

Remember, however, that only about 18 percent of Jews in Israel and only a small percentage throughout the world have any belief at all in a coming messiah. All Jews, however, desire peace with their enemies. A Muslim, regardless of his ethnic nationality, who demanded peace with Israel and produced it would be hailed as a hero by both Jews and Gentiles throughout the world.

Anytime it looks as though someone is capable of bringing peace to the region, it is suggested that this is the messiah. After the 1993 peace accords were signed in Washington, one Jewish rabbi was so hopeful that he even hailed Yasser Arafat as the promised messiah!

HE WILL RISE FROM THE MIDDLE EAST

The Antichrist will sign a treaty for seven years and break it in the middle of the seven years (Daniel 9:27). When he breaks the covenant after 42 months, his true identity will be revealed (2 Thessalonians 2:1-6). People have offered wild conjectures about the area from where the Antichrist will arise. The top guesses are New York City, Rome and Brussels.

Again, the Bible is clear about the region of the world from which this man will rise. According to Daniel and his key to understanding his prophecies, there are only four possible regions from which the Antichrist could arise. Daniel 2, 7 and 8 give us insight into the fourth kingdom that will rule the earth.

Most scholars agree that the fourth beast of Daniel's vision is none other than the Roman Empire. According to Daniel, this empire (Rome) would be divided into two parts, which historically happened when Constantine divided the Roman empire and built a city in Turkey called Constantinople. Both Constantinople and Rome were major cities in the Roman Empire.

In the 10th century, the Holy Roman Empire divided into two parts. The Orthodox Church split off and formed its headquarters in Constantinople (now Instanbul), Turkey). The Catholic Church continued to be headquartered in Rome.

The struggle for power has created tension between Rome and Turkey for almost 1,500 years. The Ottoman Turkish Empire ruled the Holy Land for 400 years—until the British liberated the area in 1917. In Daniel 2, there are 10 toes on the image, and they represent 10 kings that shall arise at the end of days.

These 10 kings are seen in another vision in Daniel, when he writes, "the ten horns are the head of the beast" (see Daniel 7:20, 24). At the end of days, 10 kings will form this kingdom of the Beast. Five must be from the western branch (Rome) and five from the eastern branch (Turkey). According to Scripture, three major events will transpire in the days of these 10 kings.

1) The Antichrist will overthrow three of the 10 kings that will arise.

> I considered the horns, and, behold, there came up among them another little horn, before whom there were three of the first horns plucked up by the roots and behold, in this horn were the eyes of a man, and a mouth speaking great things (Daniel 7:8).

The early church fathers believed that the three kings (nations) the Antichrist would overthrow are Egypt, Lybia and Ethiopia. Daniel indicates the Antichrist will take over these three nations located in the northern horn of Africa, and control them for 42 months. Hippolytus wrote:

> In those times, then he (the Antichrist) shall arise and meet them. And when he has overmastered three horns out of the ten in the array of war, and has rooted out, viz., Egypt, and Lybia, and Ethiopia, and got their spoils and trappings and has brought the remaining horns which suffer into subjection, he will begin to be God as master of the whole world.

Daniel's prophecy was the foundation for this belief:

> But he shall have power over the treasures of gold and of silver, and over all the precious things of Egypt: and the Libyans and the Ethiopians shall be at his steps (Daniel 11:43).

By seizing control of the northern horn of Africa, the sea lanes which are a conduit for hauling oil from the Persian Gulf region will be in the hands of the Antichrist. No ship can enter or exit the Suez Canal in Egypt without the permission of this dictator. Who controls this vital region of the world can dictate cargo shipments in the Middle East and along the Gulf of Aqaba, a lifeline to Israel's food and produce.

The Gulf of Aquaba is shared by Israel, Jordan, Egypt and Saudi Arabia. Much of the vegetable and fruit produce grown in Israel is presently being harvested in numerous farms in the Arabah, a strip of land about 120 miles long and 8 to 20 miles wide, extending from the Dead Sea to Aqaba. Closing the ports of Aqaba would cut off a lifeline to Israel from the south.

2) The 10 kings will give their kingdoms over to the Antichrist for 42 months.

> And the ten horns which thou sawest are ten kings, which have received no kingdom as yet; but receive power as kings one hour with the beast (Revelation 17:12).

Both Daniel and John saw the rise of 10 end-time kingdoms ruled by 10 kings. These 10 kings submit to the will of the Antichrist, more than likely out of fear. Remember that this wicked leader will be invincible in war. The inhabitants on earth will ask, "Who can make war against the beast?" (Revelation 13:4).

John informs us that these 10 kings will hand their kingdoms and their authority over to the beast (Antichrist) in one hour (Revelation 17:12). Imagine, in one hour the man who is the Beast will be given supreme authority over 10 major nations. I believe the submission of these 10 leaders will come about because of fear.

Once the Islamic nations of Egypt, Libya and Ethiopia have fallen, other Muslim leaders will have no strength to resist this person. Fear of war or retaliation will motivate the leaders to simply agree with the Antichrist's principles of war and destruction.

Today, one can observe how most of the Islamic nations unite together when one is under attack. Although it may appear from their histories that they hate each other, because they are Muslim, they will unite to destroy Israel and overthrow the dominance of the West.

3) The Lord will return to earth in the days of the 10 kings.

> And in the days of these kings shall the God of heaven set up a kingdom, which shall never be destroyed (Daniel 2:44).

> But the saints of the most High God shall take the kingdom (Daniel 7:18).

This is the most exciting part of the prophecy. When these 10 kings set up their kingdoms on earth, Christ will be preparing His final plans to set up His visible kingdom in Jerusalem!

This is why students of prophecy are excited to see the European Union unite in the area of the old Roman Empire, and observe the collapse of peace promises not worth the paper and ink they are written on. To the informed prophetic student, these recent events are a preview of what is to come.

THE ANTICHRIST WILL CONTROL THE MIDDLE EAST AND MUCH OF EUROPE

Daniel continues to close in on the area from which the Antichrist will arise. Historically, the Babylonian Empire fell into the hands of the Medes and Persians. Both the Babylonians and the Media-Persians ruled from Babylon during the time of the prophet Daniel.

After much time, the Media-Persian Empire fell into the hands of Alexander the Great, the leader of the Grecian Empire! The Grecian Empire was represented by the symbol of a ram, or male goat:

> And the rough goat is the king of Grecia: and the great horn that is between his eyes is the first king (Daniel 8:21).

Daniel predicted that the Grecian Empire would fall and be divided into four parts. He saw the horn (kingdom) of the goat divide into four regions:

> Therefore the he goat waxed very great: and when he was
> strong, the great horn was broken; and for it came up four
> notable ones toward the four winds of heaven (Daniel 8:8).

The leader of the Grecian Empire, Alexander the Great, died drunk in Babylon. His kingdom was divided among his four main generals, or as Daniel saw it, among the "four winds" (the four points of the compass: north, south, east and west). Here are the names of Alexander's four generals who took possession of the four divisions of the Grecian Empire:

1. Ptolemy took Egypt and the southern part of the empire.

2. Cassander took Greece, Macedon, and the western part.

3. Seleucus took Babylon, Syria, Iran, Iraq and the eastern part.

4. Lysimachus took Turkey, Thrace and the northern part of the empire (*Dake's Bible*, "Notes on Daniel," page 877).

Daniel makes it clear that the Antichrist, identified as the little horn (Daniel 7:8 and 8:9), would arise out of one of these four divisions of the Grecian Empire.

> And out of one of them came forth a little horn, which waxed
> exceeding great, toward the south, and toward the east,
> and toward the pleasant land (Daniel 8:9).

Daniel gives the reader four choices for the rise of the final world dictator: the area of modern Egypt, Turkey, Greece, or the regions of Syria (and Iraq, which includes portions of ancient Babylon). This is emphasized again in chapter eight, where Daniel is told that the male goat

> is the king of Grecia: and the great horn that is between
> his eyes is the first king. Now that being broken, whereas
> four stood up for it, four kingdoms shall stand up out of
> the nation, but not in his power (Daniel 8:21, 22).

Again, this alludes to the division of the kingdom after the death of Alexander the Great. The four choices we are given, then, are Egypt, Syria, Greece or Turkey.

The Antichrist will be great toward the south. This is the area of Egypt. His greatness comes after he overthrows the northern horn of Africa. He will also be great toward the east. The east is Jordan, Iran, Iraq and the land toward Afghanistan, Pakistan and the predominantly Islamic states of the southern Soviet Union. He will be great "toward the pleasant land"—a Hebrew phrase for the land of Israel.

> And in the latter time of their kingdom, when the trans-
> gressors are come to full, a king of fierce countenance, and
> understanding dark sentences, shall stand up (Daniel 8:23).

This is the Antichrist that Daniel said would "destroy the mighty and the holy people, cause craft to prosper and by peace shall destroy many. He will also come against the Prince of princes and be destroyed without hand" (vv. 24, 25).

After much study, I believe the best and most Biblical area for the Antichrist to arise is the area of ancient Assyria. This encompasses Lebanon, Syria and Iraq, or the region of the old Babylonian Empire. For example, Egypt, Libya and Ethiopia will be uprooted by the Antichrist; therefore, he does not rule from that area in the beginning. The "king of the north" will "come against him" in a war and he will go forth to cause great wars (Daniel 11:40-41).

Therefore, his kingdom is not centered in Turkey, since Turkey will become the king of the north during the tribulation. The only areas left are Greece and Assyria. Old Testament prophecies indicate trouble comes from Assyria:

> Be not afraid of the Assyrian; he shall smite thee with the
> rod, and shall lift up his staff against thee after the man-
> ner of Egypt. For yet a little while, and the indignation
> shall cease, and mine anger in their destruction.
>
> And it shall come to pass in that day that his burden shall
> be taken away from off thy shoulder and his yoke from off
> thy neck, and the yoke shall be destroyed because of the
> anointing (Isaiah 10:24-27).

> In that day also he shall come even to thee from Assyria, and from the fortified cities, and from the fortress even to the river, and from sea to sea, and from mountain to mountain (Micah 7:12).

To summarize, the Antichrist will rise from ancient Assyria—an area consisting of Lebanon, Syria and Iraq, and once the stronghold of the Babylonian Empire. Taking a small remnant of people, he will become great (see Daniel 11:23). He appears in the name of peace and signs a 7-year agreement with many nations, including Israel (Daniel 9:27). This agreement is called a covenant.

In the middle of the seven years, he will break the agreement, invade Northern Africa and seize Egypt, Lybia, and Ethiopia (Daniel 11:43). He will engage weapons of mass destruction to destroy many and, through fear, 10 nations will yield to his total authority:

> And the ten horns which thou sawest are ten kings, which have received no kingdom as yet; but receive power as kings one hour with the beast. These have one mind, and shall give their power and strength unto the beast (Revelation 17:12, 13).

A comprehensive peace treaty will be signed for seven years. In the middle of this, the Antichrist will take over control of northern Africa and invade Israel, perhaps with a united Muslim army and with the full support of the Palestinians in Israel, taking possession of East Jerusalem and all Jewish sites within the surrounding environs.

COMPARING DANIEL WITH REVELATION

1. Both saw a final period of seven years.

   • Daniel spoke of this as one week in 9:27.

   • John divided up the events of Revelation: 42 months and 42 months, or seven years.

2. Both saw a final 42 months of world history.
   - Daniel called the period in Hebrew, time, times and the dividing of time (Daniel 12:7).
   - John said it would last 1,260 days, or three and a half years (Revelation 12:6).

3. Both identified the Antichrist as a beast.
   - Daniel saw him as the fourth beast rising (Daniel 7:7).
   - John saw this beast rising from the sea (Revelation 13:1).

4. Both reveal a time of great trouble on earth.
   - Daniel said it was a time such as never was nor shall be (Daniel 12:1).
   - John described it as wrath and trouble (Revelation 12:7-10).

5. Both prophets saw Michael the archangel.
   - Daniel saw Michael standing up at the time of trouble (Daniel 12:1).
   - John saw Michael warring Satan in heaven (Revelation 12:7).

6. Both saw the resurrection of the dead.
   - Daniel saw the event after the tribulation (Daniel 12:2).
   - John saw a resurrection of Tribulation saints (Revelation 7:9-17).

7. Both prophets saw 10 kings that would arise at the end of days.
   - Daniel said the 10 horns were 10 kings (Daniel 7:24).
   - John saw 10 horns, along with 10 crowns; or 10 kings (Revelation 13:1).

8. Both prophets saw the return of the Lord at the conclusion of the Tribulation.
   - Daniel saw an everlasting kingdom (Daniel 7:13,14).
   - John saw the Lord Jesus Christ returning to make war (Revelation 19:11).

FITTING THE IMAGERY OF THE BEAST KINGDOM

Muslims receive their spiritual instruction through the Koran, which contains the statements and revelations of their prophet, Mohammed; and through the *Hadith*, a book containing the statements attributed to Mohammed. According to the Hadith, the faithful are told:

> You will fight against the Jews and you will kill them until even a stone would say, "Come here, Muslim, there is a Jew (hiding himself behind me); kill him."

The Hadith teaches, "Let Allah destroy the Jews." Such statements, and many others, place the Jews and the nation of Israel at the top of Islam's hit list.

In the religion of Islam there are two "houses," or groups of people on earth today. Muslims belong to Dar al Islam (The House of Islam), and all others in the world belong to Dar al Harb (The House of War). Fanatics believe this war against the infidel, called a jihad (holy war), is God's way of punishing the unbeliever. Therefore, unbelievers must be either beaten into submission or killed.

What group is interested in controlling Judea, Samaria and half of Jerusalem? Not just the Palestinian people, but the entire Islamic world. Many Palestinian friends who live in Israel have told me privately that they would rather be under Israeli occupation than under the control of the corrupt Palestinian Authority. One of several reasons is that Israel gives the Palestinian Christians total liberty to attend church and learn the gospel, but the Palestinian Authority, with its radical element, often attempts to persecute Arab Christians and block Christians teachings in the territories.

A MAN IN THE CIA

Years ago my father pastored in Arlington, Virginia. During that time, Dad received a telephone call from a woman who asked him to pray for her unsaved husband who was suffering from cancer. As Dad ministered to the man, he was healed and converted to Christ.

Dad later discovered that this man had a high position in the CIA. He could speak seven languages and had traveled throughout the world, including many of the Islamic nations, warning their leaders and exposing the plans of Russia. This man warned the king of one Arabian nation that the Russians were secretly training a mentally retarded nephew to kill him. Months later, while eating dinner, the nephew took a knife and killed the king who had been warned.

He also traveled to Iran and worked with the Shah of Iran. He and others had gathered information that a radical leader in exile named Khomeini was making plans to overthrow the Shah. Khomeini was smuggling in cassette tapes with his message and having them distributed among the population of Iran.

BILL'S TWO WARNINGS FOR AMERICA

This agent, whose first name was Bill, sounded a warning in the early 1970's during the time of the Arab oil embargo and after the Yom Kippur war in Israel. Bill's uncanny predictions seem more possible now than ever. He said:

> We believe it is very possible that a chemical or biological element will be placed in the water supply in America, and that could take out an entire city in a short period of time.

The second warning was more ominous, especially in light of September 11, 2001. He said:

> In the future, the greatest threat to America will be the radical Muslim terrorists from areas such as Iran. It will be a matter of time until they will have chemical and nuclear weapons in their possession. We can foresee a time when they will fly a plane over a major city and crash it into buildings, or smuggle a nuclear device into a major city

and detonate it, possibly killing hundreds of thousands of people. They will one day hold entire nations hostage with weapons of mass destruction in order to get their way.

Having traveled to these Islamic countries, Bill was greatly troubled by the fact that the United States was allowing Muslims with fanatical, anti-Israeli and anti-Western ideas to enter the country with student visas and sit in our universities. Often they would marry American women in order to obtain a permanent visa

Others simply remained in the country when their student visas ran out, blending among the thousands of other Middle Eastern citizens in America. Bill predicted that the hour would come when the freedoms of America would be attacked and the routine of our daily lives would be permanently disrupted. And he predicted these things many years before the changes occurred in once moderate Muslim nations, such as Iran.

In the early 1970s, many Islamic nations were friendly toward the West. After all, American and British drilling technology had made the Arab Gulf states rich through oil exports. Nations once friendly toward the West began to change governmental leaders in that decade, especially during the decade when Israel won the Yom Kippur War in 1973.

The fact that America sent equipment into Israel from Germany and the weapons helped Israel win the war caused anger in the Islamic world. Today, militant Islamic nations seek the destruction of "the great satan," or America.

I was preaching near a major military base in America, and teaching about how the prophecies from Daniel relate to the Antichrist and the Islamic connection. I told how, in 1995, a Professor Black in Israel told me the reason Rabin wanted peace with the Palestinians was the fear that an Arab leader would one day unite Iran, Iraq, Syria and Lebanon under one national military and political influence.

After the service, a high ranking officer in the United States military spoke with me. He said, "I want to confirm your opinion relating to a man uniting Iran, Iraq, Syria and Lebanon. I have been training with the Israelis, and I can confirm that America and Israel's greatest threat is that a radical Muslim leader will unite this area and gain possession of weapons of mass destruction."

In Louisville, Kentucky, a gentleman related to me that his friend from Iran had recently returned to the country to visit his family. He was shocked to see how the Iranians and the Iraqis had suddenly forgotten years of bloodshed and hatred and were beginning to consider uniting to strengthen their base and terror networks.

THE ANTICHRIST WILL ATTACK ISRAEL AND CONTROL JERUSALEM

Comparing Scripture with Scripture, we can get a better idea of the religious background of the future Antichrist:

- He will invade Israel after he wins a war in Northern Africa (Daniel 11:42-44).
- He will invade Jerusalem and control the Temple Mount (Revelation 13:1, 2).
- He will persecute Jews and those who receive Christ (Revelation 20:4).
- He will divide the land of Israel for gain (Daniel 11:39).

After hearing teaching on the Antichrist for many years, I began to realize that one major group of people were never mentioned in prophetic preaching. Ministers spoke of Israel and the Jews, along with the Common Market and Europe. It seemed no one was giving prophetic insight on how 1.2 billion Muslims fit into the prophetic picture.

I was also unsure how Muslims fit into Biblical prophecies until I met a young Iranian woman who gave me some astonishing information that I had never read or heard taught. The puzzle began to come together for me.

Years ago, while ministering in Baton Rouge, Louisiana, I met Ellie, a young woman from Iran. She was a Christian, but her family members were Shiite Muslims. During a revival I preached from Revelation 13, emphasizing the Antichrist and the false prophet.

After the service, Ellie approached me and asked if I had heard the teaching about the last Islamic prophet who was to appear at the end of days. I said I had not. Later that evening, she gave me some astonishing information. To understand this theory, however, it is necessary to examine the history of the Islamic religion.

Four

REVELATIONS IN THE ARABIAN DESERT

But though we, or an angel from heaven, preach any other gospel unto you than that which we have preached unto you, let him be accursed (Galatians 1:8).

For about 2,500 hundred years, the world was void of a written revelation from God. From the creation of Adam to the time of the Exodus, there was no written Scripture from God. Prior to the flood of Noah, men lived to be over 900 years of age, and they handed down information by word of mouth from father to son (Genesis 5:3-32). Finally, the prophet Moses led the Hebrew nation out of Egyptian slavery and toward the Promised Land (Israel).

A hike to the top of Mount Sinai brought the world the first written revelation from God! This revelation, called the *Torah* and penned by Moses, comprises the first five books in the English Bible. The Torah contains the Law which came directly from God while Moses was on Mount Sinai during a 40-day fast (Exodus 34:2-38). The Bible indicates the location of Mount Sinai is in Arabia (see Galatians 4:25).

For centuries, the traditional site of Mount Sinai was believed to be in the Negev desert, a large strip of rugged, rocky mountains located between Israel and Egypt. Often, tourists are shown the Saint Catherine's Monastery that allegedly marks the famous site. Some tour guides admit that this is not the true Mount Sinai, but the monastery was built as a convenience to serve the many tourists.

In the New Testament, the apostle Paul spoke about Mount Sinai. A former Pharisee, Paul was converted to Christ while traveling to Damascus, Syria. Following his conversion, he spent three years in the region of Arabia, where he received the full revelation of Jesus Christ (Galatians 1:17, 18). Paul wrote that Mount Sinai was in Arabia (Galatians 4:25). The rugged mountain area of Arabia has not changed over the centuries. It is a mass of land that includes part of Jordan, Syria and Saudi Arabia.

In the New Testament, the Apostle Paul penned seven major revelations he received from the Lord. I believe he received these while in Arabia on the same mountain, Mount Sinai, where Moses, centuries before, had received the Torah! This is why Paul went to Arabia to spent time in God's presence shortly after his conversion (Galatians 1:17, 18).

MOUNT SINAI IN ARABIA

One of the first revelations Paul received while in Arabia, I believe, is included in the first letter he wrote to the church at Thessalonica. The Book of 1 Thessalonians, the first of Paul's 14 letters in the New Testament, mentions the coming of the Lord five times. It specifically reveals an event called the "gathering together," or the "rapture" (1 Thessalonians 4:16-18).

In the book, *The Gold of Exodus*, the author tells a fascinating story of a trip to Saudi Arabia in search of the real Mount Sinai. After they experienced a series of hindrances, they secretly visited this area and took exclusive pictures of the mountain.

They noticed that the top of the mountain was burned, indicating the place where they believe the Lord came down with fire (see Exodus 19:18).On the edge of the rocky slope was a large single stone split down the middle. Closer examination indicated evidence of a dried water bed that once flowed through the large rock.

The researchers were inclined to believe this was the rock Moses smote where the water flowed, making provision in the wilderness for the children of Israel (Numbers 20:8). The importance of the mountains of Arabia is also known in the founding of one of the largest and fastest growing religions in earth, the Islamic religion.

A New Revelation From Arabia

Mohammed, the founder of the Islamic religion, was from Arabia. He claimed he saw a series of visions and revelations that became the basis for the Islamic holy book called the Koran. Mohammed, meaning "the praised one," was born in the year 570 A.D. Mohammed was from the Quraysh tribe, who claimed to be direct descendants from Abraham through his son, Ishmael.

Mohammed's father, Abdullah, died before Mohammed was born. His mother, Amina, died when Mohammed was six. He was raised by his uncle, and traveled with caravans throughout Syria and Arabia. At age 25, he married a wealthy widow named Khadija and had six children through her.

Mohammed lived near Mecca, a settlement in Arabia. It was a community situated at the crossroads of the main north/south and east/west caravan routes. Arabian merchants filled the area with beds, food, stables for camels, and other services. Mecca also contained a 140 feet deep well with crystal clear water, which drew people from far and near to Mecca. Called Zam Zam, the well was believed to cure illnesses.

The other distinguishing mark of Mecca was a large black rock, different from all others in the area. No one knew how it got there, and the caravans were afraid of it. (It was probably a meteorite.) Those living in Mecca built a large cube-shaped stone building over the rock called the Ka'ba (meaning "cube" in Arabic). The local people charged visitors for the privilege of kissing the rock for good luck. Before Mohammed's time, Mecca had become a tourist attraction for caravans. Each year pilgrims traveled to Mecca to drink from the special springs and kiss the black stone. On the stone, the inhabitants of Mecca had placed different gods and goddesses. The pilgrimages were so popular that a large stone building was erected around the Ka'ba itself.

By the fifth century, the members of the tribe of Quraysh were the guardians of the Ka'ba and were the dominant tribe in Mecca. They provided the arrangements for all pilgrims visiting the Ka'ba, and the senior members of the group collected income from the pilgrims. At the time of Mohammed, there were 360 different idols sitting on the black stone in the Ka'ba, and Mohammed's grandfather was the keeper of the keys to the Ka'ba. This was the setting in Mecca at the time Mohammed began praying and fasting.

As Mohammed grew older, he spent time on the hills outside the city of Mecca. In 610 A.D., when Mohammed was 40, he claimed to have heard a voice speaking to him while praying in a cave above Mecca. Fearful, he ran home where his wife wrapped him in a blanket. Later, he heard the voice again. This time, he said, the voice told him that he was the chosen messenger of God to bring his people, the Arabs, the message of one God who controlled all things. Allegedly, he heard the voice saying, "You, wrapped in your mantle, arise and warn."

According to Muslim beliefs, Mohammed then received a series of visions from an angel whom he said was Gabriel. The early messages consisted of God's goodness and power, the need to return to God, and the final judgement. He declared there was only one God and his name (in Arabic) was Allah. It was believed that Allah was the same God worshiped by both Jews and Christians.

As Mohammed preached his messages among the Arabs, those who chose to follow his teaching became known as Muslims and the religion was called Islam, which means submission. During Mohammed's time, there was much idol worship throughout Arabia. There were theological divisions among Christians, and the Jews and Christians were at odds with each other.

In the Arabian city of Mecca, a conflict arose among the merchants at the Ka'ba. If the people believed there was only one God, it would destroy the pilgrimages and the income from visitors who came to pray before their god. Many Arabs called Mohammed a liar, a fraud and a false prophet.

Eventually, Mohammed and his new followers were forced from Mecca and moved to a new city where they were received. Mohammed named the city Medinat-Nabi, meaning "city of the prophet." Today, it is called Medina in Saudi Arabia.

Soon a conflict arose between followers of Mohammed in Medina and the people of Mecca. Muslim groups began raiding the traveling caravans. Mohammed began teaching that if his followers died fighting, they would go straight to paradise. The 8-year war finally ceased when the people in Mecca surrendered to the Muslims. Mohammed declared Allah the true God, removed the idols, and made Mecca the center for the Islamic religion.

He continued the pilgrimages to the Ka'ba and today one of the five pillars of Islam is that Muslims must pray at the Ka'ba in Mecca at least one time before they die. This is called the *Hajj*. Through many wars and battles, the Islamic religion began to sweep through Arabia. More Arabs began joining the new religion.

At age 62, Mohammed began complaining of severe headaches and fever. Some Muslims believe he was poisoned by one of his wives who was Jewish. He never recovered and, after saying a few prayers, he passed away. During his lifetime, the followers of Mohammed acclaimed him as a prophet. He brought forth a series of what believers called "revelations."

After the death of Mohammed, his revelations were collected by various individuals, and placed in a book called the *Koran*. The Koran is considered the sacred revelation of Islam, just as the Bible is considered God's sacred revelation to religious Jews and Christians. The Koran contains 114 suras or chapters, starting with the longest sura and ending with the shortest. The suras consist of the revelations given to Mohammed over a 22-year period.

Mohammed was believed to be illiterate; therefore, his followers wrote down the revelations as they heard him recite them. The words were written on leaves, pieces of parchment, and even dried bones. The Koran was compiled after Mohammed's death, and written in the Arabic language.

Muslims believe that 104 sacred books were given by God to mankind. A hundred of these were given to Adam, Seth, Enoch and Abraham, and have been lost. The four remaining books are the books of Moses (the Torah), the Psalms of David and the four Gospels of Christ.

Most Muslims today believe the Jews and Christians changed the words in the Bible to suit their own ideas and beliefs. Several Muslims have told me they believe the Bible cannot be trusted because it was changed. There are so many translations, they say, so how can it be the true Word of God? Another book called the Hadith (traditions) is said to contain the teachings of Mohammed as they were put together by his followers who knew him personally and spent time with him.

Fourteen hundred years after Mohammed, Islam claims about 1.5 billion followers, and is the fastest growing religion in the world. Part of this is due to the fact that a Muslim man can have five wives at a time, and they often have very large families, some with 10 to 20 children. While Muslims claim to accept the Torah, Psalms, and the four Gospels, they claim the Bible has been *tahrif*, meaning "corrupted or altered." Muslims believe that since Jesus himself did not write the Bible, it is not accurate.

Many stories in the Koran are very different from the stories in the Bible. For example, the Bible teaches that Abraham dwelt by the trees of Mamre and built an altar there to the Lord (Genesis 13:18). In the Koran, it teaches that Abraham said, "O our Lord! I have made some of my offspring to dwell in a valley without cultivation, by thy Sacred House (Ka'ba) in order, O our Lord that they may establish regular prayers" (Sura 14:37).

When asking a Muslim about this contradiction between Mamre in Hebron and Ka'ba in Arabia, a Muslim said, "The Koran in infallible. The Jews and Christians changed the Bible to make it fit themselves." This is why witnessing to Muslims simply by quoting Scripture seldom wins them to Christ. It is love and the presence of the Holy Spirit that can impact their hearts.

This book is not intended to debate the doctrines of Islam. However, one will not understand how Islam will fulfill many of the Bible's predictions of an eighth kingdom that seeks to destroy Israel and the Jews unless one understands certain Islamic beliefs and traditions.

MOHAMMED'S DEATH AND THE
TWO BRANCHES OF ISLAM

The death of Mohammed left a void in the leadership of the Islamic religion. He announced no successor; therefore, the battle for top position began immediately. Muslim elders elected Mohammed's second convert and the oldest man in the group, Abu Bakr. Abu's title was *caliph*. Most Muslims accepted this decision, but a small minority did not. The smaller group believed Ali, Mohammed's adopted son and the father of Mohammed's two grandsons, Hassan and Hussein, should be the leader. A struggle began that led to the deaths of many of Islam's first caliphs.

The Sunnis and the Shiites became the two branches of Islam, with the Sunnis accepting Abu as successor and the Shiites believing Mohammed's successor was Ali. Abu Bakr, the first caliph, brought the tribes of Arabia under Islamic rule. The second caliph, Omar (634-644), began an expansion that lasted for 100 years. Under Omar, the mosque in Jerusalem was built on the Temple Mount.

During this 100 years, Muslim armies extended the empire into Iraq, Iran and parts of Central Asia. As Syria came under Islamic control, the headquarters of the Umayyad Dynasty (661-750) was Damascus, Syria. The third caliph, Othman, was assassinated, precipitating a war between the Sunni and the Shiite Muslims that continues to this day.

As the years progressed, several different Islamic dynasties arose. The headquarters of the Shiites eventually became Baghdad, Iraq. In Karballa, Iraq, Hussein, the son of Ali, was murdered, along with 70 followers. Each year during the Islamic month of Muharram, the Shiites commemorate the death of Ali.

This division not only split the religion into two branches, it caused a split about where the headquarters should be.

While all Muslims consider Mecca and Medina to be sacred places, the Sunnis claimed Mecca as their headquarters and the Shiites moved from Damascus to Baghdad. Today Tehran, Iran, has become the stronghold of the Shiite branch.

Eventually the division became so great that 11 of the 12 early Shiite leaders were poisoned or killed by their opposition. According to Shiite belief, the 12th leader will play a role at the end of days. This 12th holy man was the 12-year-old son of the 11th Imam. At age 12, this young boy, destined to be a chosen Imam of the Shiite branch, disappeared off the street in his city and was never found.

It is this missing Imam and Islam's strong belief that he will re-appear in the last days that will pave the road for multitudes of Middle Eastern Muslims to accept a future man as their final prophet. The power and influence of this man will climax with the takeover of much of Israel, the division of Jerusalem and the death of many Jews and Christians who will not convert to Islam. It was this Islamic teaching of the last days that opened my understanding of the revelation of Biblical prophets concerning the time of the end.

ISLAM AND THE LAST DAYS

It comes as a surprise to many Christians to learn that Muslims have strong traditions about the "last days." Oddly, their expectations of what will happen parallel the Biblical predictions of a final world empire controlled by a war-like military leader. In Israel, I have met with both former and practicing Muslims to compile many of their beliefs relating to the last days.

In the Koran the last days are noted by several terms: the day of uprising, the day of separation, the day of reckoning, the day of awakening and sending forth, the last day, the encompassing day, and the hour. Many Muslims teach that the last days will be preceded by three blasts of a trumpet:

- ♦ At the first blast, all creatures in heaven and earth will be struck by terror.
- ♦ At the second blast, all creatures in heaven and earth will die.
- ♦ At the last blast, 40 years later, all will be raised again for the judgement.

The length of judgement will be 1,000 years (some Islamic scholars say 50,000 years).

ISLAM'S FINAL PROPHET, THE MAHDI

If you ask Muslims if they believe in Jesus, they will reply, "Of course." If you ask them if they believe Christ will return one day, they will again reply "yes." But their concept of Jesus and His return is far different than what the Scripture teaches. The Jesus of Islam is a Muslim who will return and help convert the world to the Islamic religion.

Years ago, I was amazed to discover that Muslims believe they will one day control the entire world and that everyone will eventually become a Muslim. I was also disturbed to discover what most Muslims felt about Jews and the state of Israel, especially among those Muslims living in the Middle East.

The Shiites have a teaching called the Doctrine of the Twelve. It states that after Mohammed, there were 11 caliphs. The 12th was the son of the 11th, and he disappeared when he was a young boy.

Since the graves of the other 11 are known and the grave of the 12th has never been discovered, the tradition states that the 12th caliph has been supernaturally protected by Allah for the past 1,200 years. Most say he is in a desert in Arabia. Still others believe he is being preserved in Iraq.

Since the disappearance of the 12th Imam in 878 A.D., Muslims have been expecting a final prophet to appear. He is called the Mahdi and will lead a last-days Islamic revival. This man, according to tradition, will be a military expert who will bring the world under the control of Islamic law and justice.

The Shiites, which is the more radical group, are placing high expectations upon the soon arrival of this prince who will conquer Israel and the West. Many will tell you that it won't be long now. This sect teaches that, at the end of days, the 12th will reappear and become the final prophet of Islam. This man is recognized in the Islamic world as the Mahdi.

THE MYSTERIOUS COMING OF IMAM AL MAHDI

The word *Mahdi* translates as "the guided one." The belief, especially among Shiites, is that the Mahdi will be guided so directly by Allah that he will be divinely protected from error and sin in all that he does. He will interpret Islam to all men and lead the final Islamic revolution that will convert the world to the religion of Islam. Shiites believe the Mahdi will be both a political and a military leader of great conquest.

There are numerous traditions concerning this mysterious person. The Islamic holy book, the Koran, has little to say concerning this man. Most traditions developed in the eighth century and beyond. While both the Sunni and the Shiite branches have a teaching on the Mahdi, the Shiites have the strongest teaching that he will appear near the end of the world. Below is a list of teachings from Islamic tradition concerning the Mahdi and the end of days:

♦ His name will be Muhammad, and he will trace his lineage as a direct descendant through Fatima, the daughter of Muhammad.

- ◆ His father and Mohammed's have the same name.
- ◆ He will have the disposition of Mohammed.
- ◆ He will have a bald forehead and a high, hooked nose.
- ◆ He will have a distinctive mole (the "mark of a prophet") and a V-shaped aperture between his front teeth.
- ◆ He will appear just before the end of the world, during a time of great difficulty.
- ◆ He will convert the world to the Islamic faith.

Most Muslims believe the Mahdi will arise from the East. Other traditions state that this man will unite Muslims in a single, united kingdom. If men do not submit to his teaching and following, he will beat them into submission until they return to Allah. Of course, those who rebel against him will meet a swift death by the sword of Islam.

Some Islamic nations still behead people for certain crimes. My father's former CIA friend was in Saudi Arabia when a group of men were buried in the sand with their heads protruding from the ground. Using a bulldozer with a sharp blade, the heads of the offenders were literally severed from their bodies and covered in the sand.

ANOTHER SET OF TRADITIONS

Other Islamic traditions indicate the areas where many Muslims believe their final leader will arise:

- ◆ The Syrian army will attack him, but will be destroyed in the desert. When this happens, both Iran and Syria will unite to pledge their allegiance to him.
- ◆ He will seize Turkey through force.
- ◆ After uniting all of Islam, he will then take over the entire world in the name of Islam.
- ◆ Muhammad predicted the conquest of Spain, which some believe will occur under the Mahdi.

- Under the Mahdi's leadership, there will be great prosperity, including gold and silver for his faithful followers.

- After all of this is accomplished, the Mahdi will rule for five, seven, or nine years (depending on which tradition is followed), and then the end of the world will come, followed by the judgement of Allah

When we study the expectations of Muslims, we find amazing parallels between their traditions of the Mahdi and the prophecies relating to the Antichrist that are revealed in the Bible. For example, compare the above Islamic traditions to Biblical references alluding to the world's final world dictator, the Antichrist.

While some Muslims would not appreciate the comparison between this expected one and the Biblical Antichrist, other Muslims who have seen this comparison are almost shocked to see the parallels between the 1,200 year old Islamic expectations and the ancient prophecies of the Bible.

The Mahdi will unite the Muslim world; and the Antichrist will bring 10 kings under his subjection (Revelation 17:12). The Mahdi will bring gold and silver to his followers; while Daniel the prophet predicted the coming Antichrist, "Will honor his god with gold and silver" (Daniel 11:38). The Mahdi, according to some traditions, will rule for seven years. The Antichrist will come to his position early during the seven-year Tribulation (Daniel 9:27).

According to Islamic beliefs the Mahdi will take over Turkey. Daniel states that the "King of the north shall come against him. The king of the north during the Tribulation will be the nation of Turkey, and Turkey will be in conflict with the Antichrist (Daniel 11:40).

Syria and Iraq will submit to the Mahdi. I believe there is Biblical evidence that the Antichrist will come out of this area, which is the territory of ancient Babylon. Most

Muslims believe the Mahdi will appear from the east. Daniel states that the coming Antichrist will be "great toward the east" (Daniel 8:9).

Muslims believe that, after the appearing of the Mahdi, Jesus will reappear and will march into Jerusalem following this Islamic leader. Then, according to Muslims, Jesus will announce He is a Muslim, and that He was not the Son of God. He will convert the people to Islam. According to tradition, this is when He will kill the "swine" (Jews) and remove the cross (referring to the killing of Christians).

The Bible indicates a false prophet will arise following the Antichrist takeover of Jerusalem, and both the Antichrist and false prophet will form a large religious following (Revelation 13:11-15).

A Muslim from Israel

I have spent quite some time questioning Muslims about their doctrine regarding the time of the end. I asked a Muslim from the Middle East (whom I will leave nameless) to sum up in a paragraph Islamic expectations for the future, involving Israel, Jesus, and the Mahdi. He said:

> In the last days there will be earthquakes, famines, and strange signs from Allah. There will come several men claiming to be prophets in the name of Allah, but they will be false. We are warned not to follow them. They will work in line with the Antichrist. Then, our Mahdi will rise to power. He will come, according to tradition, riding on a white horse. Jesus will appear and follow the Mahdi.

> We believe the Mahdi will come to Jerusalem and liberate it from the Jews and Christians. He will convert people to Islam when Jesus tells everyone that He lied, that He is not the Son of God, because God cannot have a son. Jesus will perform miracles to prove He is Jesus. He will point people to the Mahdi, and will kill the Jews and tell the

Christians to forsake the idea of the Trinity and forsake the Cross. Islamic justice will rule the earth. Those who rebel against the Mahdi will be punished, and some say with a sword. - *Interview with a Muslim from Jerusalem, November 30, 2001*

On March 8, 2002, journalist Cal Thomas wrote an opinion editorial entitled, "Where are the Sleeper Cells," in which he quoted a story from the *Washington Post* on Islamic schools in America. He said they are teaching their children that the day of judgement can't come until Jesus Christ returns to Earth, breaks the cross, and converts everyone to Islam; it can't come until Muslims start attacking Jews. The *Post* reported 200 to 300 Islamic schools nationwide, with at least 30,000 students who hear this teaching.

An 11th grade textbook used at the Islamic Saudi Academy in the Virginia suburbs of Washington teaches that one sign of the day of judgement will be when Muslims fight and kill Jews hiding behind trees and say, "Oh Muslim, oh servant of God, here is a Jew hiding behind me. Come here and kill him." It should be noted that this Islamic apocalyptic theology is not isolated to a few thousand fanatics, but is a part of the mainstream belief of Muslims throughout the world.

The Jesus that Islam teaches is far different than the Jesus of Christianity. Muslims believe Jesus was one of 25 great prophets, yet they totally deny His deity (that He is the Son of God), His death on the cross and His resurrection. The Koran teaches:

The Jews call Uzayr a son of God, and the Christians call Christ the Son of God. That is a saying from their mouths; (in this) they imitate what the unbelievers of old use to say. Allah's curse be upon them: how they are deluded away from the Truth! (Sura 9:30).

A strong emphasis of Islam is that "God is not begotten neither does he begat." A Muslim will deny that God has a son, or that He would ever have a son. The Koran puts a curse upon anyone who would confess such: "Allah's curse be upon them" (Sura 9:30). This is the strongest difference between a Muslim and a true Christian. In order to experience redemption from sin, true Christians believe Jesus is the Son of God (Colossians 2:9; Romans 1:3-4; Hebrews 1:2-3).

In the Koran, Jesus is called *Issa ibn Maryam*, meaning "Jesus Son of Mary" (Sura V:19, 75, 81, 113). One Muslim pointed out that there are about 34 direct or indirect references to Mary in the Koran. The Book of Revelation teaches that the beast will be worshiped by much of the world.

> And all that dwell upon the earth shall worship him, whose names are not written in the book of life of the Lamb slain from the foundation of the world (Revelation 13:8).

In the scriptures, a second man, idendified as the false prophet, rises to power. He will team up with the Antichrist, pointing people to worship the first Beast (the Antichrist).

THE ROLE OF THE FALSE PROPHET

> And I beheld another beast coming up out of the earth; and he had two horns like a lamb, and he spake as a dragon. And he exerciseth all the power of the first beast before him, and causeth the earth and them which dwell therein to worship the first beast, whose deadly wound was healed.
>
> And he doeth great wonders, so that he maketh fire come down from heaven on the earth in the sight of men, and deceiveth them that dwell on the earth by the means of those miracles which he had power to do in the sight of the beast; saying to them that dwell on the earth, that they should make an image to the beast, which had the wound by a sword, and did live (Revelation 13:11-14).

While our main subject in this book is the future Antichrist, this is a good time to point out that he will have a teammate who is identified with the symbolism of a lamb with two horns. Later in Revelation he is called "the false prophet" (Revelation 16:13). The Book of Revelation indicates this false prophet will team up with the Antichrist after he tramples the city of Jerusalem. Some scholars have taught that this false prophet will be accepted by many as Jesus. Several counterfeit miracles, such as calling fire from heaven and creating an image (icon) that will speak and live, will add to the deception (Revelation 13:11-16).

> And he had power to give life unto the image of the beast, that the image of the beast should both speak, and cause that as many as would not worship the image of the beast should be killed (v. 15).

If Muslims believe that both the Mehdi and Jesus will appear together in Jerusalem, kill the swine (the Jews), destroy the Cross (Christianity), and convert the world to Islam, then one can understand the meaning of John's vision in Revelation 13.

The beast rising out of the sea is the Antichrist, the coming Islamic "savior," and the false prophet will proclaim himself as Jesus by performing (Satanic) miracles to convince an already deceived humanity that He (Christ) has returned to earth to announce the truth!

This is why Paul warned about the Antichrist (the man of sin) and of the great deception through satanic miracles. "Strong delusion" will cause people to "believe a lie" and be condemned (2 Thessalonians 2:11, 12).

The amazing miracles of the false prophet will mesmerize the masses into following the Beast and joining his kingdom. Since Muslims do not believe Christ was crucified, the false prophet has no need of producing scars in his hands or his side the way Christ did after His resurrection (John 20:27).

Muslims did not get their traditions of the Mahdi or the return of Jesus from the Biblical prophets. In fact, when I share the information about the Islamic dictator with Muslims, I get two responses. One will say, "This is amazing. I never knew the Bible spoke of such things."

The other response is for the person to become defensive that I would even consider that a radical Muslim will one day fulfill the role of the Bible's predicted last world dictator. I am often told that even Muslims believe a man, similar to the Biblical Antichrist, will come and they are not to follow him. A point should be made here that not all Muslims are radical. In fact, a moderate Muslim gets along well with other people and is very friendly and considerate. Some of the most hospitable people I have met anywhere in the world are the Arab people in some parts of the Middle East.

In much of the Islamic world, especially in the Middle East, concepts and perceptions are completely different from those of Muslims I have met in Romania and Bulgaria. Muslims in the Middle East have a much more ingrained hatred for the Jews and Israel. Yet, when the subject of Israel and the Jews comes up, there seems to be a united response among moderate and fundamentalist Muslims. They believe the Jews have land that does not belong to them; it belongs to the Palestinians and the Arabs.

It was once believed that the more secular education Muslims receive, the less apt they are to become a terrorist. This was totally disproved with the 19 hijackers of September 11, 2001, as most were very well educated. It was also believed that the terror groups were mostly of the Shiite branch of Islam. This was also proven incorrect. Bin Laden and most of the Taliban were Sunni Muslims, as were most of the terrorists on September 11.

Part of this is due to the spread of radical Islam through the Iranian, or Shiite, branch. Groups such as the Palestinian Liberation Organization (P.L.O.), Hamas, and Islamic Jihad are constantly promoting terrorism against the Jews in Israel and are being motivated and sponsored by the more radical Shiite branch of the Islamic religion.

Any Muslim leader who could "liberate" Israel and Jerusalem from Jewish hands and turn Israel into an Islamic state would be hailed by all Muslims as a true prophet of Allah. He could effectively claim the title of Mahdi!

In 1979, several Islamic leaders attempted to lay claim to the position of Mahdi. I will discuss this in the next chapter.

Five

THE MAHDI,
ISLAM'S MESSIAH

Then shall they deliver you up to be afflicted, and shall
kill you: and ye shall be hated of all nations for my name's
sake (Matthew 24:9).

On November 20, 1979, some 50,000 Muslims were celebrating the 1,400th year of Islam in Mecca. As the crowds
were beginning morning prayers, a group of 350 armed men
and their followers suddenly burst into the Harem, the
Grand Mosque that encloses the Ka'ba, the large black
stone, at Islam's holiest site. They demanded that one of
their holy men, Abdullah al-Qahtani, be declared the Mahdi.

When the chief Imam refused their demands and pronounced them as heretics, fighting suddenly broke out as
50,000 worshipers were trapped in the conflict. The command was given to close and lock the 26 gates of the mosque.
Snipers rushed atop seven minarets (prayer towers).

The seige lasted for two weeks, due to certain Islamic laws relating to damaging the mosque. Also, the hostages were not to be injured and the Saudi government wanted to rescue them alive.

The fundamentalist rebels believed the time had come to cleanse Islam of influences that were corrupting it. They wanted a ban on soccer, television and higher education. After the assault ended, 63 of the rebels were beheaded, including the leader, Juhaiman.

During this 1,400[th] anniversary of Islam, an Iranian exile named Ayatollah Khomeini managed to return to his country, remove the moderate Shah of Iran, a friend of the West, and institute a radical form of Islam. Americans were shocked when the U.S. Embassy and its personnel were held hostage for 444 days.

The Ayatollah, during his exile, smuggled thousands of cassette tape messages to his followers in Iran. These messages were planting the seed for the people of Iran to receive this radical leader upon his arrival. The timing of the Ayatollah's return was also suspect. He returned on the 1,400[th] anniversary of the founding of Islam. There were high expectations that the Mahdi would rise out of Iran or a neighboring nation. Some believe Khomeini timed his return in hopes the people of Iran would declare him the final prophet, the expected one.

In 1991, prior to the Gulf War, Yasser Arafat contacted the president of Iraq, Saddam Hussein, and congratulated him for waging war on the United States. He then spoke of the glorious time when he (Arafat) would wave the Palestinian flag over Jerusalem as the capital of the new Palestinian state, and Saddam would ride his white stallion across the Mount of Olives toward the Temple Mount! Is it a coincidence, then, that many Islamic leaders own a white stallion or horse—in case Allah should chose them to be the Mahdi?

HATRED FOR THE JEWS

The first murder in the Bible was committed in the name of religion when Cain slew his brother, Abel. Both men brought offerings to the Lord, but the Lord favored Abel's sacrifice. In a jealous rage, Cain murdered his brother (see Genesis 4:5-8). Since that time, men have killed one another "in the name of God."

Jesus warned of a time when His people, the Jews, would die as martyrs, and the murderers would believe they were doing God a favor. During the past 2,000 years, the world has been drenched in the blood of innocent people who were victims of religious conflict. From the Roman Empire to the Roman church to the Inquisition to the call for Islamic Jihad, God's name has been used to murder those who disagree with another man's religion.

It has been pointed out, especially by politicians and American Muslims, that Islam is "a religion of peace." I contend there are many peaceful Muslims in parts of the world, but the history of the religion is one of war and not peace. While most Muslims are not out searching for physical combat, they all quietly believe the world needs to be converted to Islam.

One of the tenets of Islam is that of jihad, or holy war. Few Americans had heard the term *jihad* until the attack on America on September 11, 2001. Even then, for fear of anti-Arab sentiment, newscasters were reminding Americans that Islam is a peaceful religion.

Yet, few commentators quoted the Islamic scriptures that fanatical Muslims were using to teach that it is perfectly okay to slaughter innocent Americans and Jews, or the "infidels." Here are some verses from the Koran, Islam's sacred book:

> ♦ Warfare is ordained for you, though it is hateful unto you; but it may happen that you hate a thing which is good for

you, and it may happen you may love a thing that is bad for you. Allah knoweth, ye know not (2.216).

♦ Let those who follow the Gospel judge according to what God has revealed therein. Evildoers are those that do not judge according to Allah's revelations (5.47).

♦ Believers, take neither the Jews nor the Christians for your friends. They are friends with one another. Whoever among you seeks their friendship shall become one of their number. Allah does not guide the wrongdoers (5.51).

♦ Believers, do not seek the friendship of the infidels and those who were given the Book before you, who have made of your religion a jest and a diversion. Fear Allah, if you are true believers (5.57).

Notice this Koran passage about the Jews:

The Jews say: Allah's hand is fettered. Their hands are fettered and they are accursed for saying so. Nay, but both His hands are spread out wide in bounty. He bestoweth as He will. That which hath been revealed unto thee from thy Lord is certain to increase the contumacy and disbelief of many of them, and We have cast among them enmity and hatred till the Day of Resurrection. As often as they light a fire for war, Allah extinguisheth it. Their effort is for corruption in the land, and Allah loveth not corrupters (5.064).

DOES THE KORAN SPEAK OF FIGHTING AGAINST NON-MUSLIMS?

These passages from the Koran illustrate the Muslims' desire to fight against non-Muslims:

When the sacred months are over slay the idolaters wherever you find them. Arrest them, besiege them, and lie in ambush everywhere for them (9.5).

Fight against such of those to whom the Scriptures were given as believe in neither Allah nor the Last Day, who do not forbid what Allah and his apostle have forbidden, and do not embrace the true faith, until they pay tribute out of hand and are utterly subdued (9.29).

Many Muslims point out that in the 11th century, Christians from England began the Crusades to free the Middle East and Palestine from the Muslims. The Crusades were a bloody time of war and many innocent people died; yet, the Crusades do not represent the teaching of Jesus Christ and the revelation of the New Testament. Jesus taught a Gospel of peace and love. He even said to love your enemies:

> But I say unto you, Love your enemies, bless them that curse you, do good to them that hate you, and pray for them which despitefully use you, and persecute you (Matthew 5:44).

> But I say unto you which hear, Love your enemies, do good to them which hate you, bless them that curse you, and pray for them which despitefully use you. And unto him that smiteth thee on the one cheek offer also the other; and him that taketh away thy cloke forbid not to take thy coat also (Luke 6:27-29).

During recent years, fanatical Muslims have set out to murder non-Muslims, especially Christians, throughout the world. When one considers the evidence, it becomes hard for a rational person to accept the idea that Islam is a "religion of peace." It is easy to see how Muslims could apply the words from the Koran in a literal fashion and justify the murder of Christians and Jews. Just recently:

- More than 40 churches have been destroyed by Islamic extremists in northern Nigeria.
- In Lebanon, over 100,000 Arab Christians have been killed by Islamic fanatics.
- In Sudan, Muslim extremists have killed over two million Christians.
- In Indonesia, Christian churches are burned and Christians martyred by Muslim fanatics.

- In Egypt, Ethiopia and a host of other African nations, Islamic fundamentalists have challenged the government.
- In Armenia, a war between Christian Armenians and Muslim Azerbaijanis continues, with more than 35,000 casualties.
- The war in Yugoslavia was between Orthodox Serbs and Muslim Albanians.
- Even though the Philippines is 95 percent Christian, Muslim groups on Mindanao Island want an independent Islamic nation.
- India is experiencing severe clashes between Hindus and Muslims. India's population includes 200 million Muslims.

I once spoke with an Islamic leader in Israel. A friend had set up the meeting in a hotel in Jerusalem, away from cameras, tour groups and interruptions. I began questioning him about the last days, about Israel and Jerusalem, and about what he believed would be the end result. For several hours we conversed. My interpreter (a non-practicing Muslim) later told me the plans involving the non-Islamic nations.

He said that Muslims would move into and live in other nations, especially those that were friendly (including America). They would attend Western universities and marry women from the host country, thus giving them the status of a citizen (Muslims who marry an American woman can get a permanent visa). He predicted they would move into the major cities and begin to populate them by having many children. They would convert as many as possible to Islam, he said, especially among the inner city black population. (The Nation of Islam is an African-American Islamic organization.)

After building thousands of mosques and purchasing hotels, restaurants and businesses, they would become such a force or influence that no matter what happened (terrorism or otherwise), they could not be removed from the nation without a major internal war. If they went to war (a jihad) against, let's say, America, all Muslims would join in and "take out" as many as they could. This is one reason nations such as France are anti-Israel and pro-Islam in their political stance. Over six million Muslims live in France. Any political restraint against the group is met with swift opposition from a major voting block of Muslims.

Muslims have made Western Europe their first target for this type of strategy. Once the Muslim population reaches the millions, it becomes virtually impossible for a host country to support Israel or the Jewish people. Political pressure is so great and the fear that this group could unite in terrorism is so real that national leaders simply back away from appearing to support Israel. A close look at Western Europe demonstrates the fast spread of Islam. Over the past 25 years, more than 1.5 million of England's 58 million inhabitants have become followers of the Islamic religion. Over 300 Christian churches have been turned into mosques.

Seldom, if ever, does any nation on earth (except America and occasionally Great Britain) defend Israel's rights to the land. Two reasons for this lack of support are oil and the fear of terrorism. First, because western European nations have heavy Shiite populations, they understand that their entire nation could suffer irreparable damage from Muslim fanatics unleashing biochemical or nuclear weapons upon their population centers. Secondly, Arab Muslims own the oil fields and refineries. The financial base of Europe could be destroyed with a massive oil embargo similar to the one America encountered in 1973-74.

In 2000, the Islamic population in America was estimated at four million, according to an article in *U.S. News and World Report*. We recently discovered that the suicide terrorists who crashed into the Twin Towers and the Pentagon were "sleepers," a modern term for a terrorist who fits into the customs and culture of the country. Sleepers often attend college, obtain jobs and become quiet neighbors as they secretly plan to kill as many "infidel" Americans as possible. They believe they do this with the blessings of Allah.

ISLAM'S SECRET SPIRITUAL STRATEGY AGAINST AMERICA

Recently, I received a phone call from the pastor of a large church in Florida. He had just met with an Egyptian now living in America. The Egyptian, a Coptic Christian, told the pastor that if he went public with this information few people would believe him, some would resent him, and the Muslims would simply deny what he was saying. He said there are organizations that support a plan to infiltrate the Christian churches. This is the plan:

The goal of many Muslim men is not just to marry an American woman, but to marry a Christian woman. A higher goal is to marry the daughter of a Christian pastor and have children through her. Certain Islamic groups will provide secret financial support to a Muslim man who can marry a pastor's daughter. The reason: with a Muslim son-in-law, the minister will feel intimidated about supporting Israel or debating Islamic religious beliefs, for fear of offending his daughter and son-in-law. Many Christian women are impressed with the good looks, the attention and the money of Middle Eastern men.

What they often do not know is that the same man, according to Islamic teaching, can also have four other wives! At times he may say, "I am sending money to my family," and he may be. It may be his mother and father; or, in some cases, it may be another wife in another part of the country.

The second point has to do with raising the children. A true Muslim will insist that the children be raised as Muslims and be given Muslim names. Again, this can cause terrible conflict in a family. This is why the Bible teaches that, in marriage, we should not be "unequally yoked together with unbelievers" (2 Corinthians 6:14). Christian women who marry spiritual unbelievers take on a challenge that is often spiritually overwhelming. The same is true when two individuals with opposing spiritual views attempt to live under the same roof.

I know of several cases where men from the Middle East who were already married began to swoon over young women from America. Eventually they talked the women into marriage in order to receive a permanent visa to America. A few years later, they were gone, looking for their second and third wives, and leaving the women in confusion.

In the mid-1980's, I would often use Arab guides on my Holy Land tours. I became upset to discover, on returning home, that one of the guides had "dated" one of the young ladies on the trip and asked her to marry him and get him to America. The problem was that he was married with five children and did not inform her! There are rare cases when a Muslim man loves his wife and family and gives her freedom to raise the children as Christians. But from a purely Biblical perspective, a Christian should marry only a Christian (2 Corinthians 6:14).

THE GOAL: ONE RELIGION, ISLAM

We must remember that just as Christians believe they must evangelize the world with the gospel (see Matthew 24:14), Muslims also believe they are on a mission from Allah to convert the world to Islam. This is based on the belief that since God is one, He has only one religion and that religion is Islam. In the Koran, Sura 3:19, Allah says, "The only true faith in Allah's sight is Islam."

In the Muslim mind, all of the prophets, from Abraham to Jesus, were Muslims—although the religion did not originate until the 6th century. Therefore, the Koran is the final and true revelation of Allah, Mohammed is the final prophet, and the Koran is said to be written in the holy tongue of God, which is, according to Muslims, Arabic. Until a nation has embraced Islam, it is legally considered a battlefield (*Dar-ul-Harb*). Once it has been converted to Islam or all its citizens have been slaughtered or driven out, it then becomes a Land of Peace (*Dar-as Salaam*). Fanatical Muslims have a saying: "First destroy the Saturday people (the Jews), then the Sunday people (the Christians)."

Expectations of the End Days

A Turkish grand sheikh visits Kataragama, Sri Lanka, each year to look for signs of the coming Islamic savior. In an interview in the *Sunday Times*, a paper in Colombo, Sri Lanka, Shiekh Nazim Adil al-Haqqani spoke to reporter Shabuddin on events expected in the future, including the expected Islamic savior whose appearance will save the world and convert the masses to the religion of Islam:

> As believers of the traditions, we believe in a savior who will come first, before Jesus Christ. We have in our traditions his name, which is Muhammad d'ul Mahdi. He is coming but his arrival will be after a great war. It will be the fight of the big powers with each other. And in that war, the savior will come like a divine hand from heaven to stop the war.
>
> We know that this world is being prepared for huge appearances. In a short while there will be a common change, physically and then spiritually. Time is now over. All nations and all mankind are being prepared for something that is approaching soon. These are huge events—unexpected, huge events.

He referred to an interesting Islamic tradition related to where the future Islamic savior is believed to be hiding:

> There will be a great war break out between the East and the West. There will be strong fighting. Many people will be killed. Then the Lord will command al-Mahdi Alaihi as-Salam

to appear. Now he is in a cave, in a big, deep cave. No one can approach it. Jinns (genies) are protecting and guarding him.

Many Muslims, especially from the Shiite branch, believe the Mahdi is being protected and supernaturally preserved in an empty desert area in Arabia, or in Iraq. The very thought of someone hiding in a desert area reminds me of the warning Jesus gave concerning false prophets and false christs, when He said:

> Wherefore if they shall say unto you, Behold, he is in the desert; go not forth: behold, he is in the secret chambers; believe it not (Matthew 24:26).

THE OSAMA FACTOR

The name, Osama bin Laden, became a household word after September 11, 2001. Credited with the bombing of the U.S. embassies in Kenya and Tanzania, along with the suicide bombing of the U.S.S. Cole battleship in the Persian Gulf, this evil-inspired Islamic radical was able to hide in Afghan caves and train terrorists who would later fly planes into the Twin Towers and the Pentagon.

Few Americans were aware that after September 11, many of the poor, uneducated Muslims throughout the world began whispering that bin Laden may be the Mahdi. While in Charlotte, North Carolina, I was informed by a Muslim, a businessman from Iran who watches Middle East television via satellite, that some Muslims throughout the world actually believed that bin Laden fits the description of the Mahdi. The Muslims who whispered among themselves the bin Laden-Mahdi connection did so on this basis:

- ♦ Bin Laden is from Saudi Arabia, the general area from which the future messiah of Islam will originate.
- ♦ Bin Laden was willing to wage war against the world's greatest superpower in the name of Islam.

- ◆ Bin Laden was able to attack the West and bring fear into the hearts of an entire nation that he considers to be a tool of Satan.

- ◆ Bin Laden was able to hide in deep caves, both in the time of the Soviet invasion and during the war in Afghanistan, and he attacked a Western superpower from a cave.

- ◆ Bin Laden was attempting to bring "pure" Islamic justice to Afghanistan.

- ◆ He was standing against the "corrupt" royal families of Saudi Arabia, while demanding the removal of Jews from Palestinian land.

This combination struck a cord in the hearts of many Muslims. American and British television seldom reports these things, but Arabic television aired by satellite throughout the world constantly promotes hatred toward Israel and the Jews. It regularly blasts the West for being a friend of the Jews. In Kenya, East Africa, three major Islamic networks air their propaganda throughout the city and the nation. All networks propagate hatred toward Israel and the Jews. Some are even antagonistic toward the West.

Because of bin Laden's unknown whereabouts for months, some Muslims believed he would re-emerge at an appointed time and unite a massive following that would shake the West. Obviously there is a hunger in the Islamic world for this Mahdi to soon appear, defeat the Jews and Christians, and convert the world. Most Muslims recognize that the defeat of the West and global control can be accomplished only through war and the use of weapons of mass destruction.

It is possible that bin Laden has been injured or killed. If not, he will certainly be killed or caught in the future. His is the most noted face in the world. Yet, he is a miniature preview of the coming Antichrist who will fulfill Biblical prophecies as well as the expectations of Muslims who have their own prophetic traditions.

APOCALYPTIC MUSLIMS

Why would Islamic radicals select this present time to target the United States? Part of the explanation may be the prophetic timing of certain Islamic traditions. According to Sheik Nazim, he met the 39th sheik in the Golden Chain that began with the Prophet Mohammed 50 years ago in Damascus, Syria. Presently, this chain is in the 40th generation, and the Muslims believe that the Mahdi is the descendant of the Holy Prophet (*Sal*) from the 40th generation.

This prophetic expectation is causing excitement among many Muslims. It is breeding anticipation that the great hour of Islam lies just over the horizon. Ayatollah Janati, a leading Islamic cleric in the Iranian government, has stated several times: "The 21st century will be the century of Islam."

In Israel, an Arab friend whose family is Muslim told me of a tradition he had heard for years. One of the traditions of Mohammed is that when tall buildings begin to fall to the ground, it is a sign of the last days and the Mahdi will soon appear. While my friend and his associates had heard this for years, they did not have anything in writing that said when or where the tradition originated.

One CIA agent reported to a dear friend that the men who hit the Twin Towers and the Pentagon could be classified as "apocalyptic Muslims." The term "apocalyptic Muslim" defines a Muslim who believes his actions will help bring about the fulfillment of the signs of the end time, thus expediting the appearance of the Mahdi and the conversion of the world.

A friend whose team was on location after the Pentagon attack stated that the body of one of the terrorists who flew the plane into the Pentagon was later discovered in the ruins. Portions of his body were mutilated and he was strapped in the pilot's seat with a cloth covering his body. This cloth was a death cloth that an Islamic martyr uses prior to his death; it prepares the Islamic martyr to enter paradise. The same type of cloth is wrapped around the loins of men who prepare for a suicide bombing.

The secular news media often says the terrorism against America occurred because of our support for Israel and our policies in the world. This may be the political reason, but the underlying, hidden motivation is spiritual. It is the belief that the West and its culture must be defeated because its Christian culture keeps the influence of other religions from gaining a stronghold. When we see the mind set of apocalyptic terrorists, nothing makes logical sense.

The question lingers: why kill innocent people when moderate Muslims say the Koran forbids it?

The Hadith says that Mohammed saw a woman who had been killed in a battle. According to tradition, he said, women and children should not be killed in conflict. Why brainwash young children to become a human bomb in an act of suicide against common people who have done you no harm? Why is it impossible to negotiate and reason with a terrorist? Because they are convinced that death for Allah and for the cause of Jihad will guarantee entrance into heaven.

The June 2, 2002 National Weekly Edition of the *Washington Times* described how a Palestinian mother dresses her 12-year old son in the homemade costume of a suicide bomber, complete with a small kaffiyeh, a belt of electrical tape, and fake explosives made of plywood. "I encourage him to do this," said the mother of six. "God gave him to me to defend our land. Palestinian women must have more and more children until we liberate our land. This is a holy duty for all Palestinian people." Her son said, "I hope to be a martyr. I hope when I get to be 14 or 15 to explode myself."

This brings to mind something Attorney General John Ashcroft said in a speech after the September 11 attacks. He said, "One of the differences between Islam and Christianity is that in Islam, their god expects you to send your son to die for him. In Christianity, God sent His son to die for you."

THE 72 VIRGINS

I have interviewed Muslims in Israel about why some strap on explosives and become a human bomb. From these interviews I've detected three major keys that motivate a handsome young Muslim to offer himself as a martyr on the altar of Allah.

1. Death is better than their present living conditions. Most young suicide bombers live in refugee camps. Living conditions are terrible, and there is little hope for joy in this life. Instead of blaming the rich oil states for not assisting them financially, they put the blame on Israel, which then becomes the target. At the time of this writing, Saddam Hussein is contributing $10,000 in cash to the parents of any child who serves as a human bomb. In the Gaza paper, the family will often thank Saddam directly for his financial gift for the family.

2. Guarantee of heaven for their families. When a young man blows himself up, the mother will often go on television, hail her son as a hero and praise Allah for the great honor of allowing him to die a martyr for the cause of Islam. This puzzles those in the West, especially mothers who cannot imagine a son dying in such a manner.

In the mind of the Islamic fanatic, however, he has guaranteed his entire family, as well as himself, entrance into paradise. There he will be hosted by Islamic leaders, including the prophet Mohammed himself. Recent evidence indicates the families of the bombers are well provided for, with a guarantee of $5,000 to $25,000 for the sacrifice of their child as a martyr.

3. The 72 virgins await him. Every Islamic fanatic who sacrifices himself and kills enemies believes he will awake in paradise and enjoy 72 virgins who will have sex with him throughout eternity. Prior to a suicide attack, a young man will cover himself with a white shroud and go through an elaborate ritual. This sick, perverted way of thinking is high motivation for recruiting new terrorists.

A Muslim friend in Israel tells me that suicide terrorists actually lie awake in bed at night and spend hours fantasizing about the possibility of 72 perfect women waiting in rooms in paradise to bring pleasure to those who die in a jihad for Allah. The 72 virgins and the guarantee of entering paradise strongly motivates young men to blow themselves up and take as many "infidels" with them as possible.

But what about the motivation for a female suicide bomber? Is she promised 72 young men? The answer may lie in the fact that huge amounts of money are given to the families of those who will die a martyr for Islam. Saddam Hussein handed out checks for $10,000 to the families whose children would die while killing Jews in Israel.

In 2000, Saddam raised the benefits for Palestinian martydom to $25,000 per family. Since the average Palestinian makes only a few hundred dollars a year, this is an appealing offer. No wonder they brag on their dead child and hail him as a "hero." The unfortunate youth has just provided many years of financial security for the family!

WHITE RAISINS

There may be a strange twist related to the fantasy about the 72 virgins. Those who have studied the Koran have noted that Mohammed had contact with Jews and Christians living in Arabia. Some of the stories in the Koran are from the Bible, and some include Christian and Jewish legends that were popular in the time of Mohammed.

John Wansbrough of the School of Oriental and African Studies in London believed that the Koran was a series of voices or texts compiled over a longer period of many years.

There is no evidence that the Koran ever existed until A.D. 691, or 59 years after Mohammed's death. This was about the time the Dome of the Rock was built in Jerusalem. Even the inscriptions inside the Dome, according to Dr. Wansbrough, differ somewhat from the present Koranic text.

Christoph Luximburg from Germany's Sarrland University has studied early copies of the Koran, and notes that vowel and dot points were added to the Koran in the 8th and 9th centuries, similar to the way the old Hebrew alphabet placed dots beneath the letters to demonstrate the vowel sounds. The passage that speaks of the virgins is the word *hur*. Islamic traditionalists say the word is *houri*, meaning "virgin." But Luximburg notes that according to early Arabic language and one early Arabic dictionary, the word *hur* means "white."

In researching, he discovered that the passage in the Koran is similar to a fourth century passage written in a Christian document called "Hymns of Paradise." The passage speaks of paradise having flowing rivers of water, fruit trees and white raisins. In early times in Arabia, white raisins were considered a delicacy and were highly prized. It could be that Mohammed spoke of white raisins being in paradise and not virgins. How disappointing this must be to a suicide bomber!

AT-PLO PORK BULLETS

While many snicker at the idea that young men would believe their martyrdom would pave the way for an eternity in paradise with 72 virgins, another belief concerning pork could keep the bomber out of his anticipated eternal dwelling. Neither religious Jews nor Muslims are permitted to eat pork. According to Samuel E. Driben, a Jewish colonel in the U.S. Marine Corps, fervent religious Muslims believe that contact with swine can kill their souls. In the Koran and in the Hadith, contact with swine products could actually deprive

Muslims of Paradise: "Allah has forbidden you carrion, blood, and the flesh of swine" (Sura 2:173).

During the Spanish-American War of 1898, American forces in the Philippines were attacked by the Moros, a fanatical suicide group who believed Muslims could gain entrance into Paradise by dying in a jihad against an "infidel." Documents from that period show that captured Moros were greatly afraid of any contact with pork. During the war, thousands of pork skins were obtained; and many of the captured Moros were wrapped and imprisoned in the pork skins. Many of those killed were buried in pork flesh. Eventually, word began to spread among the Moros and they began losing their desire for terrorism.

Several years ago after studying this strange strategy, a chemist by the name of Rabbi Moshe Antelman developed a pork laced bullet that he believed could restrain much of the uprising inside of Israel, especially among the extreme fanatics. He believed his bullets, code named AT-PLO (Anti-terrorist Paradise Lost Ordinance) projectiles, could take the momentum out of would-be terrorists.

The theory is that if a Muslim believes that through contacting pork he could void his entrance into Paradise, then make the pork bullets available. Let the terrorists know that if they attack innocent people, they will be shot with pork bullets. Or if they act as a suicide bomber, their remains will be wrapped in pork and buried in the ground.

The latter scenario actually did occur in Israel. When a suicide bomber blew himself up in Northern Israel, several men from the community obtained pork, took the pieces of the terrorist's body, and wrapped it in the swine's flesh and buried it. The Muslim leaders within Israel went into a rage. After the men in the Jewish community buried the remains of the Islamic militant in pork skin, they were asked why they did this. Their answer was, "Any person who would blow himself up and thinks he gets 72 virgins certainly thinks pork would keep him out of heaven. We're just helping him stay out."

It should be noted that some secular Muslims do not believe the story of the 72 virgins in paradise, nor are they overly concerned about the issue of pork. Several years ago the Israeli army was interested in the idea of using pork projectiles against terrorists, but the upper brass of Israel was concerned about the repercussions within Israel and abroad among the Muslim community. However, Jews who have built settlements in areas near the Gaza strip are interested in the pork bullets, or any other types of ammunition.

After hearing this, someone suggested that America could have saved millions of dollars in the war in Afghanistan if the U.S. military would have flown thousands of pigs into the mountains where the al Qaeda fighters were hiding, and allowed the animals to run wild through the caves and across the mountains. Of course, such a wild strategy would have brought the wrath of the Islamic world against the United States and would have unsettled the people of Afghanistan.

By the way, the November 1, 2002 *Wall Street Journal* carried this item by columnist James Taranto:

> According to the *Moskovski Komsomol* newspaper, Russian security forces have decided to bury the terrorists from last's week's hostage siege wrapped in pig's skin. The aim is to deter potential Islamic terrorists from future attacks.

LAND OF THE ASSASSINS

Despite the foolishness of the theory, the belief in 72 virgins is a powerful motivation for a poor, illiterate young man with no hope for the future. The desire to become a human bomb can be traced to a concept rooted among the Shiite Muslims of Iran, especially a cult known as the

Assassins. Led by Hasan-i-Sabbah, the group flourished from about 1090 A.D. until 1256 A.D. Their headquarters was in the rugged Elburz Mountains, in the stronghold of Alamut.

Known as Nizari Isamailis, the group believed that Ali was the true heir to Mohammed, along with two of his descendants, Ismail and Nizar. The Isamailis were terrorists in the truest form, willing to die for their leader, Hasan-i-Sabba. The first written information about the Ismailis was reported by Marco Polo. This famous traveler first called the group the *hashishin*, meaning "an eater of hashish." This error in the name may have originated from the concept that Sabbah used to mix a special potion with the drug hashish prior to a follower enacting a murderous assignment against his enemy.

The sad part, according to Polo, was that Sabbah's armies of assassins were young boys from the ages of 12 to 20. Most were the sons of poor simple-minded people who were seduced by the high-profile charismatic leader. Sabbah would expound on the wonderful life that awaited in paradise for those who accepted martyrdom. Their leader would use the drugs to bring his future assassins into a drug-induced state, thus convincing them of the wonderful feelings they would have in paradise.

According to Polo, Sabbah would say:

> Go thou and slay so and so; and when thou returnest my angels shall bear thee into Paradise. And should'st thou die, nevertheless even so I will send my angels to carry thee back into Paradise (*The Travels of Marco Polo*).

The same spirit that inspired Sabbah to sacrifice young boys for his cause also inspired leaders such as the late Ayatollah Khomeini and even Saddam Hussein to offer their youth as human shields and sacrifices for Allah. Such events occurred during the 10-year war between Iraq and Iran. The border between the countries was filled with dangerous land mines. In order to spare the top soldiers from a tragic death, plastic keys were tied around the necks of thousands of young boys, who were sent into the land mines in order to clear the field for their army. They were given the plastic key so that, upon their deaths, the key would fit the gates of paradise.

Inside Israel, Palestinian schools teach young children more than reading and writing. There are areas designed to promote the concept of martyrdom in the name of Islam for the cause of jihad against Israelis.

While having lunch, one Palestinian friend told me, "Those who are going to blow themselves up literally sit around all day and fantasize about the *hoor al-ain*, the virgins of paradise. They conjure up images of how each virgin will look and the acts they will perform."

The revelations coming out of the Arabian desert in the sixth century are far different from the Biblical truth that was birthed on Mount Sinai through Moses and confirmed by the Apostle Paul. The Bible is a book containing thousands of prophecies. While the parallels between the Islamic Mahdi and the future Beast are amazing, there is much more evidence from the Scriptures. To support this theory, let's look at some important clues from the Biblical prophets.

Six

CLUES FROM THE BIBLICAL PROPHETS

Surely the Lord God will do nothing, but he revealeth his
secret unto his servants the prophets (Amos 3:7).

It is the Bible that gives accurate, inspired prophecies
relating to future events. As we explore Daniel's predictions, along with the book of Revelation, many amazing
parallels connect the prophecies of Daniel with John's
apocalyptic vision. In light of our recent understanding of
a final Islamic Kingdom, these prophecies can now be understood clearly.

Few Christians have been taught the information you have
been reading. Prophetic teachers often interpret the Scriptures through the lens of traditional Western customs and
culture. Some prophetic teachers have never visited Israel,
do not understand Middle Eastern customs and religious
beliefs, and certainly have omitted the world's 1.2 billion
Muslims from the prophetic picture. Therefore, some of what

you are reading may go against the grain of tradition. I challenge people to weigh this information in light of Scriptures, instead of through handed-down Western theology. Often we need to re-examine our theology and be willing to adjust when we receive more light on a subject.

Several years ago, I was teaching on "The Islamic Beast Theory" at a major prophetic conference. One man said, "Perry, your teaching on the Islamic beast makes more sense than anything I have heard. Yet, I can't teach this. I have too many books out there that teach something else."

I jokingly told this teacher that in 1978, as a teenage preacher, I knew who the Antichrist was until they shot him; then I had to change my teaching. I also had to tell folks that I was wrong. I was preaching what other people were saying, instead of researching the Word and comparing Scripture with Scripture.

The Ultimate Goal

The ultimate plan of Islam is to unite the world in a global world order under the control of Islam. Some in the West (America) think this is an unreachable goal, but consider that Islam is the fastest growing religion in the Middle East and Europe. Although forced conversion is part of Islam's plan, this is not the reason for its growth. It is the fastest growing religion because a Muslim can have five wives, and often one family may have 10-20 children per household. The average contemporary family in the West may have two children, while Muslims believe in large families.

Muslims see Israel as a thorn in their side. Many are taught that Abraham was a Muslim and the Jews have no historical right to the Temple Mount. Therefore, Jews are infidels and must be removed from the land. As we search the Scriptures and examine passages dealing with the last days, the Antichrist and the coming Tribulation, it is amazing to see how prophets painted a picture, thousands of years ago, that connects the prophetic puzzle to the Islamic religion as the final world empire. It shows the Antichrist as a warring Islamic leader.

Israel is the only non-Muslim nation in the Middle East. The final battle will be Armageddon, a 200 square mile valley located in the heart of Israel. Israel's enemies will march toward Jerusalem at the conclusion of the Tribulation, only to be destroyed by the brightness of Christ's coming (2 Thessalonians 2:8).

JOHN SAW SOMEONE RIDE IN ON A WHITE HORSE.

Muslims have told me on several occasions that the final Islamic prophet, the Mahdi, will arrive riding on a white horse. In John's vision, at the beginning of the seven-year Tribulation, he saw a rider on a white horse galloping upon the world scene. This appears to be a military leader as he carries a bow, a weapon used in ancient wars.

> And I saw, and behold a white horse: and he that sat on him had a bow; and a crown was given unto him: and he went forth conquering and to conquer (Revelation 6:2).

Because of the tradition of the Mahdi and the white horse, some Islamic leaders own a special white stallion, in case Allah should raise them up as the Mahdi. Two of these leaders include Colonel Moamar Qaddafi of Lybia, and Saddam Hussein of Iraq.

THE ANTICHRIST RULES WITH A GREAT SWORD.

The prophetic Scriptures indicate that the coming world dictator will be a violently aggressive military leader. His war-like character is alluded to in another passage penned in John's end-time vision in the Book of Revelation:

> And there went out another horse that was red: and power was given to him that sat thereon to take peace from the earth, and that they should kill one another: and there was given unto him a great sword (Revelation 6:4).

This passage speaks of events at the beginning of the 7-year Tribulation. Scholars note that the color red is a symbol of war. In the original Greek, the phrase "great sword" is *megalee machara*. The root word for *megalee* is *megas,* meaning "exceedingly large or great." "Sword" comes from the root word *mache* , a word alluding to fighting, striving or battling.

According to Islamic tradition, one of the three items the Mahdi will restore will be the sword of the prophet Mohammed. This sword will enable the Mahdi to exact Islamic justice, especially on infidels who resist his leadership. The sword of Islam also alludes to jihad, or a holy war that can be called against the infidels.

The color red is also interesting because of an Islamic tradition involving dying martyrs in a jihad. During the war between Iraq and Iran, Ayatollah Khomeini needed to clear the land mines on a battlefield. He gave a call and 10,000 young boys, some as young as eight and others as old as 13, answered the call for jihad. The Ayatollah then strapped red tape across the forehead of these youths and gave each a plastic key he named the "key to paradise."

The children, now ready to open the doors of paradise with plastic keys, ran into the field, blowing themselves apart, so that the older soldiers could cross the field and fight the opposing army. The red tape, a visible marking on their foreheads, showed their desire to die for Allah.

A passenger on the doomed flight that crashed in Pennsylvania on September 11, 2001, called his wife from the plane. He described the hijackers as Middle Eastern men wearing red headbands and holding a red box they claimed was a bomb. Red cloth is often connected to fanatical Muslims who desire to die as martyrs.

Could the red horse with a great sword in Revelation allude to the so-called jihad, or sword of Islam, being called against the world? This prophetic horse and rider "takes peace" from the earth (Revelation 6:4). The red horse and rider is seen in John's vision early in the Tribulation. The Bible says, "They should kill one another" (Revelation 6:4). Certainly this is a picture of modern fanatical jihad.

It is interesting to note that after this rider, the Bible then speaks of many martyrs who are in heaven crying out for vengeance (Revelation 6:9-11). Apparently, these are people who are killed in the Tribulation because they had received Christ and were not willing to follow the teaching and laws of the Antichrist.

THE PALE HORSE AND RIDER ARE SEEN.

Early in the first 42 months of the Tribulation, John saw the imagery of another horse and rider. The English translation of the Bible identifies this horse as "pale."

> And I looked, and behold a pale horse: and his name that sat on him was Death, and Hell followed with him. And power was given unto them over the fourth part of the earth, to kill with sword, and with hunger, and with death, and with the beasts of the earth (Revelation 6:8).

The word "pale" is the Greek word *chloros* and is translated in two passages, Revelation 8:7 and 9:4, as the word *green.* Literally, this horse is green in color. While in Israel I noticed there were fluorescent green lights placed around the upper part of all the mosques. At night, the green glow can be seen miles away. I assumed these glowing green lights were simply to draw attention to the mosque as the centerpiece of the community.

I later learned that the color green was considered to be the color of the prophet Mohammed, because it was the color of the earth. This same color, green, is found on many flags in Islamic nations, including the Palestinian Liberation Organization (PLO), Turkey and other nations. This pale or green horse will march through the earth bringing death and hunger to entire nations.

This rider is also given power to kill with the sword, which throughout the Scriptures represents war. Could this green horse be a reference to the influence of Islam to create war during the early part of the Tribulation? As stated earlier, the verses following the pale horse speak about a large number of martyrs who are in heaven crying out for vengeance upon those who murdered them on earth. Later, in Revelation 20:4, it is revealed they were murdered by beheading, which is a common practice among the more strict Muslims.

DEAD BODIES WILL LIE IN THE STREETS FOR $3^{1/2}$ DAYS.

After Antichrist invades Jerusalem, he will kill two prophets of God identified as the two witnesses (Revelation 11:3). Many scholars, along with early church writers, believe these two witnesses are Elijah and Enoch, the two men who never died (see 2 Kings 2:11-12 and Hebrews 11:5).

The Antichrist will become a hero in the eyes of Islam when he takes control of Jerusalem and the Temple Mount. At this point, he will set himself up as God (see 2 Thessalonians 2:4).

The Antichrist will also kill the two witnesses and leave their bodies in the open street for over three days:

> And their dead bodies shall lie in the street of the great city, which spiritually is called Sodom and Egypt, where also our Lord was crucified. And they of the people and kindreds and tongues and nations shall see their dead bodies three days and an half, and shall not suffer their dead bodies to be put in the grave (Revelation 11:8, 9).

Muslim nations have been known to hang people for certain types of crimes. In the 1990s, an Assembly of God pastor in Iran was arrested and publicly hung. It is assumed this could be how these two witnesses are killed. In Israel, Orthodox Jews bury people the same day they die; they avoid the embalming process. I have been on the Mount of Olives when two large buses filled with Orthodox Jews would stop and people would jump off the bus and follow a truck with a corpse in the back. Within a few minutes, the final prayers were offered and the dead person was buried.

The same tradition exists among Muslims. They attempt to bury the departed on the same day the person dies. The only exception is a non-Muslim who has been killed for blaspheming Islam, or a political enemy who has been executed. Years ago in Syria, an Israeli spy was hung and his body allowed to be kept in the open for several days so people could spit on him and curse the Jewish spy. It appears the same action will be taken against these two witnesses. They will be so feared and despised that upon their death, people will not permit them a normal burial.

For three and a half days, or about 74 hours, their bodies will lie exposed in the street. The reason could be the fact that the Antichrist will become a hero in the Islamic world when he invades Jerusalem and annexes the entire area of East Jerusalem for his new capital. To see the bodies of his enemies lie in the street will bring such joy that people will send presents to one another (see Revelation 11:10). A proud Islamic militant would allow the bodies of these men to rot in the street while his followers rejoice over a "liberated Jerusalem."

PEOPLE WILL BE BEHEADED DURING THE TRIBULATION.

As previously mentioned, the Scriptures indicate that the method used to kill anyone who will not worship or follow the future beast will be execution by beheading:

> And I saw the souls of them that were beheaded for the witness of Jesus, and for the Word of God, and which had not worshiped the beast, neither had received his mark upon their foreheads, or in their hands; and they lived and reigned with Christ a thousand years (Revelation 20:4).

The Greek word used here for "beheaded" comes from a root word *pelekus*, meaning "an ax." It alludes to a person whose head is removed by another using an ax. This small passage may give us another clue to the Islamic thread and the Antichrist.

It is common in strict Islamic nations for a person who has committed a high crime to be beheaded. Certain crimes, such as stealing, are punishable by cutting off the right hand. This punishment was used recently by the Taliban in Afghanistan. Eyewitnesses state there would often be a basket full of hands sitting next to a man holding a sword. Those accused of stealing had their right hand removed by the sword.

Even in the Israeli West Bank communities, young women who were accused of adultery have been stoned to death with their parents' permission. Those accused of higher crimes are executed by beheading. This has been done in Saudi Arabia. Beheadings have occurred in Indonesia and parts of Latin America by using an ax, and in some Islamic nations by using a sword.

Therefore, Islam is the one major world religion that in many areas still practices execution and punishment using the "sword." In the Tribulation, those resisting the Antichrist, rejecting the mark of the beast (see Revelation 13:16-18) and refusing to worship his image will be met with the swift death of beheading. As noted, those killed by beheading may be the martyrs recorded in Revelation 6:9-11. These various clues add evidence to the theory that the Antichrist is a Muslim.

The Antichrist Will Set his Headquarters in Jerusalem.

And he shall plant the tabernacles of his palace between the seas in the glorious holy mountain; yet he shall come to his end, and none shall help him (Daniel 11:45).

Since the Six Day War of 1967, the Arab world has attempted to "liberate Jerusalem" from the hands of the Jews. While the Temple Mount and the two mosques, the Dome of the Rock and the Al Aqsa, are in the possession and control of the Muslim authorities, the Muslim belief is that Jerusalem should be the capital of a Palestinian state and should be liberated from Jews and Christians.

The more secular Muslims are not as dogmatic, but the majority of Middle Eastern Muslims demand that the Jews lose their grip on Islam's third holiest city, Jerusalem. When the Antichrist takes control of Jerusalem, the city will once again be divided, as before 1967, and a war to exterminate the Jews will continue unrestrained for 42 months:

> For I will gather all nations against Jerusalem to battle; and the city shall be taken, and the houses rifled, and the women ravished; and half of the city shall go forth into captivity, and the residue of the people shall not be cut off from the city (Zechariah 14:2).

> But the court which is without the temple leave out, and measure it not; for it is given unto the Gentiles: and the holy city shall they tread under foot forty and two months (Revelation 11:2).

Before 1967, Jerusalem was divided between east and west Jerusalem. The eastern section was the country of Jordan and the western section was Israel. A large concrete wall topped with barbed wire served as a cold, hard reminder of the sharp division between Arab and Jew. After the Six Day War in 1967, Israel removed the wall and annexed east and west together as one city. This was the early stages of a fulfillment of prophecy in Psalms 102:16, stating that "When the Lord shall build up Zion, then he shall appear in his glory."

Since 1967, the Palestinians have fought an internal battle for total control of Jerusalem. They see Israel as an invader, and America as a supporter of the infidel Jews. The terror attacks from inside Israel are meant to build opposition against Israel as the great oppressor of the Palestinians. The Palestinians claim they were there first and the Jews are illegally occupying Palestine.

Yet, a travel guide to Palestine published in 1906 by Karl Beadeker states the population of Jerusalem at 60,000, of whom 7,000 were Muslims, 13,000 were Christians, and 40,000 were Jews. This survey was made when the Islamic Ottoman Empire (Turkey) was ruling! Prior to the formation of Israel in 1948, the Arab and Turkish Muslims got along quite well with the Jews living in Palestine. It was the formation of Israel in 1948 that changed the atmosphere.

The re-establishment of Israel brought fear to the Muslim world, and the reunification of Jerusalem brought anger. Since 1948, Israel and Jerusalem have become centerpieces of controversy. Since Muslims do not believe the Jewish Temples of King Solomon and King Herod ever sat on the Temple Mount, "The Night Journey" story tells them that they alone should control the holy mountain of Mohammed.

The controversy of Jerusalem and the Temple Mount will be the flame that ignites a fiery conflict inside Israel. The one group that demands the departure of the Jews from Jerusalem is the Muslims.

> *Question*: With whom is Israel trying to make peace?
>
> *Answer*: The Islamic world, including the Palestinians, the Syrians and other Islamic nations.
>
> *Question*: Who lays claim to Jerusalem?
>
> *Answer*: Three world religions: Islam, Christianity, and Judaism.
>
> *Question*: Who would attempt to stop the building of a Jewish Temple in Jerusalem?
>
> *Answer*: Islam. Muslims consider Jerusalem to be the third holiest site of their religion.
>
> *Question*: What world religion still uses a sword to punish people who sin against their religion?
>
> *Answer*: Fanatical Islam. In certain countries, if you steal, they cut off your hand.

Question: What global religion still practices beheading people?

Answer: Islam. Under certain crimes, people are beheaded, as they will be during the Tribulation.

Question: If Jews are "fleeing" during the Tribulation, and Christians are being beheaded for their testimony, then what Gentile religion could reclaim control over Jerusalem?

Answer: Islam and over a billion Muslims around the world.

The Antichrist will set himself up as God in a future rebuilt Jewish Temple. Paul wrote, "He as God will sit in the temple of God, showing himself that he is God" (2 Thessalonians 2:4). When the radical Islamic leader takes over Egypt, Libya, and Ethiopia, he will then invade Jerusalem to "liberate" the Temple Mount from the hands of Jews. Any Muslim who could "liberate" Jerusalem from Jewish control would be a hero to Muslims across the world.

THE GREATEST CLUE TO THE MYSTERY

After studying the connection between the Islamic traditions of the Mahdi and the strange link to the Biblical end-time prophecy, I realized the greatest clue that ties the links together is John's description and definition of the Antichrist. John says that the Antichrist will deny Jesus is the Son of God (1 John 2:22). One of the major rifts between Islam and true Christianity is over who Jesus was and is.

Islam teaches that Jesus was born of Mary and was a great prophet but that He is not the Son of God. The Koran teaches that God is not begotton and neither does He begat. True Christianity, on the other hand, declares Jesus is the Son of the living God! John said the person (or spirit) that denies the relationship of Jesus and the Father is antichrist! While most Muslims consider Christians heretics for believing Jesus is the Son of God, the Bible states it is the Antichrist spirit that denies Jesus is the Son of God. Certainly Islam denies Jesus is God's Son!

THE IRANIAN CONNECTION

Presently, Iran is the strongest radical Shiite Muslim stronghold in the world. Iran desires to eventually take over the country of Iraq. During the Gulf War, the reason our government restrained itself from assassinating Saddam Hussein was his hatred for Iran. Saddam has actually served as a buffer between the radicals of Iran and the nation of Israel. In fact, for several years, America supported Saddam and assisted in building up his military. Then, he became offended at America and turned against the West.

The desire of the Iranians to take over Iraq may be for more reasons than just seizing more oil reserves and positioning armies closer to Israel. It appears to be rooted in the concept that the Mahdi may reappear in present-day Iraq. To the Shiite Muslims, Iraq is an important place with its past and future history. After the death of Mohammed, both Damascus, Syria and Baghdad, Iraq became the two headquarters for Shiite Islam.

- ◆ Many years ago the headquarters for Shiite Islam was Baghdad, Iraq. The Shiites could make this city the headquarters of the Shiite branch of Islam.

- ◆ The city of Karballa is in Iraq. Karballa is a holy city to the Shiites. It is where Al-Hussien, the grandson of Mohammed was murdered, along with 70 of his followers. The Shiites consider Hussien to be the true heir of the prophet Mohammed.

- ◆ The city of Samarrah is located in Iraq. This is allegedly the city where the 12th Imam was born and the city, some believe, where he will reappear in the last days.

- ◆ This 12th imam disappeared and his grave was never discovered.

Eventually, Iraq will fall to radical Islam. There may be a time of change after the death of Saddam Hussein, but it will be brief. Others note that Saddam has several sons who desire to take control of Iraq after their father's death. A son who is in exile in Germany, said in a 1998 interview that if he took power the world would wish his dad was still in charge. He said he would be worse than Hitler!

Once the radical Muslims control Iraq, they will have Syria in their back pocket. Lebanon was once an Arab Christian nation; but when the fanatical Muslims took over the nation, many Arab Christians were forced to flee the country. Some were permitted into Israel and others had to face severe persecution and even death at the hands of terrorists. For many years, the Iraqis, Syrians and Lebanese have been predominantly Sunni Muslim. It has been in the mind of the Shiite Muslims to control the governments of Iraq, Lebanon, and Syria and form an Islamic crescent that would include Israel.

The Shiite branch is quite different from the Sunni branch in several aspects:

- Many Shiite Muslims are heavily involved in occult activities. They accept palm reading and the reading of tea leaves. There is even a secret group that pierces their bodies with swords and do not bleed. One girl saw a man place three nails in his head, and there was no blood. This was not a trick.

- The Shiite Muslims often have pictures of their Imams, which the Sunnis do not. It would not be difficult to see a group of Shiite Muslims, along with a group of apostate Christians, worshiping the image of the beast that is brought to life through the demonic powers of the false prophet (Revelation 13:11-15).

- The Shiites have a strong desire to take Jerusalem and destroy Israel. They are the group that constantly calls for a jihad against Israel.

There are three simple reasons why I believe that out of a strong fanatical branch of Islam will come a man who will hold the world hostage with nuclear, chemical, and biological weapons. It also appears likely he will come from the Shiite branch of Islam.

1. The world's final dictator will become "great with a small people" (Daniel 11:23). The Shiites make up only about 18-20 percent of the Islamic population.

2. Daniel also indicates that he will be "great toward the east" (Daniel 8:9). East of Jerusalem, Israel are the countries of Iraq, Iran, Afghanistan, Pakistan and the southern Russian states. These territories are the stronghold of the more militant and radical Muslims. Iran is about 98 percent Shiite Muslim.

3. While many Sunni Muslims have Jewish friends and get along very well with Christians from the West, the Middle Eastern Shiite Muslims have a tendency to be overtly anti-Semitic. Many consider America to be "the great satan."

A strange twist was that bin Laden and many members of al-Qaeda were Sunni Muslims. I have heard Sunni Muslims in Israel and America say that the way the radicals act is not true Islamic teaching and is a perversion of the traditions. One Sunni in Israel told me, "I hate the Shiites. They give everyone a bad name."

Recent events in light of Bible prophecy give us amazing clues as to how events will unfold in the near future. Without a doubt, Israel, the Jews and the Temple Mount will play the leading role in end-time prophecy.

Seven

TEMPLE MOUNT, THE WORLD'S HOT SPOT

Behold, I will make Jerusalem a cup of trembling unto all the people round about, when they shall be in the siege both against Judah and against Jerusalem (Zechariah 12:2).

No real estate on earth, except the Temple Mount in Jerusalem, is reverenced by more than two billion people representing three major religions! Controversy over this 50-acre property can and has sparked riots leading to deaths on the mountain itself. It is ground zero for a future war, foretold in the Bible, that will rock the world.

Israel's land mass is about the size of New Jersey. Jerusalem itself is about the size of Knoxville, Tennessee. The ancient city has been destroyed and rebuilt numerous times in history—twice when the Hebrew nation was attacked in 606 B.C. and A.D. 70. The city has changed hands eight times during the past 1,900 years. Islam's interest in the city goes back to the tradition of a night journey by Mohammed.

Muslims cite a vague sura or chapter in the Koran titled "The Night Journey." The first verse alleges that one night Mohammed took a journey on his horse, Barrak, and traveled "from the Sacred Temple to the Farther Temple, whose surroundings we have blessed, that we might show him some of our signs." It is said that he met with Moses, Elijah, Jesus and a host of other prophets. Afterwards, he ascended into heaven on his horse, journeying back to Arabia.

In the seventh century, the Muslims began teaching that the two temples referred to in The Night Journey were located in Mecca and Jerusalem. Today, when visiting inside the Dome of the Rock Mosque in Jerusalem, Muslim guides show visitors a natural indentation in the rock, alleging that it is the footprint of Mohammed's horse when he flew from this site back to Arabia.

After the death of Mohammed, Caliph Omar went to Jerusalem and built the Dome of the Rock. It received its name because of the golden dome that glimmers in the sun and the fact that the building sits over a large stone, often called the foundation stone of creation. The El Asqa mosque and Dome of the Rock have become the third holiest site in Islam.

It should be pointed out, however, that Jerusalem is never mentioned by name in the Koran. Some scholars even doubt that the alleged night journey ever took place in Jerusalem, and that this tradition developed after the death of Mohammed. The Koran mentions Mecca hundreds of times, but it never mentions Jerusalem. Still, most Muslims believe the story.

The Secret of the Dome of the Rock

In a recent controversial book titled *Secrets of the Dome of the Rock*, author Yacob Ofir researched evidence in which he alleges that the Dome of the Rock was originally used as a house of prayer for the Jewish people. Others have pointed out that the Dome of the Rock is an eight-sided mosque; therefore, the shape is not in the tradition of an Islamic mosque. Even the entrance to the mosque is on the western side. Nonetheless, after both mosques were built, the Temple Mount was eternally marked for Islam. According to Islamic teaching, once a mosque is built on a site, it becomes the property of Islam for eternity.

In the eyes of millions of loyal Muslims, the presence of Jews and Christians in a city where the third holiest mosque sits borderlines on blasphemy. These attitudes became visible when American troops, pouring into Saudi Arabia to protect the oil fields, were forbidden to wear any cross or visible emblem of Christianity. They were initially forbidden to bring Bibles into the region. Stiff opposition from Americans, including the outspoken Senator Jesse Helms, brought about a reluctant change of decision by the Saudis.

Other nations, such as Iran and Iraq, demanded that the infidel American and foreign troops be expelled from Arabia, since Saudi Arabia is the home of Mecca and Medina, Islam's two holiest cities.

This is said to be one reason bin Laden planned the attacks against America. It was a message of hatred for Americans going into Arabia during the war. Little is made of the fact that bin Laden, the son of a billionaire, had a $250 million inheritance from his father and that his family made much money by rebuilding roads and buildings after the Gulf War.

Joseph Telushkin wrote in *Jewish Literacy*:

> Orthodox Jews pray three times a day for the Temple's restoration. During the centuries the Muslims controlled Palestine, two mosques were built on the site of the Jewish Temple. (This was no coincidence; it is a common Islamic custom to build mosques on the sites of other people's holy places.) Since any attempt to level these mosques would lead to an international Muslim holy war (*jihad*) against Israel, the Temple cannot be rebuilt in the foreseeable future.

During the Six-Day War in 1967, the Israelis reunited the divided city of Jerusalem. For a brief time the Temple Mount was in the hands of the Israelis. An Israeli flag was hoisted above the Western Wall as Israelis danced below. Shortly thereafter, General Moshe Dayan gave the keys of the Temple Mount gates to the Islamic Waqk.

Some Jews feared that Israel's control of the sacred mountain and the two mosques would ignite an all-out war with surrounding Islamic nations. Even Jews were not permitted to pray on the Mount, an order that was enforced by Israeli soldiers. Since 1967 the Temple Mount has been the undisputed mountain of Islam. Recently, fear that the Jews would one day capture the Mount and build a Jewish Temple have caused the Muslims to make secret plans that are now being discussed more openly.

DOME OF THE ROCK—A FUTURE JEWISH TEMPLE?

For centuries scholars have noted the prophecies regarding a future Jewish Temple on the Temple Mount. The references are found in three places in the New Testament:

> He as God will sit in the temple of God showing himself that he is God (2 Thessalonians 2:4).

> Measure the temple of God and they that dwell therein, but the court that is without, leave out, for it is given to the Gentiles and they shall tread down the city for forty two months (Revelation 11:1, 2).

With the destruction of two Jewish Temples (in 606 B.C. and A.D. 70) and the fact that two Islamic mosques now sit in Jerusalem, many scholars interpret these passages in a spiritual or an allegorical manner. They teach that the temple is the human body, or the body of Christ (the church), and that the enemy will attempt a final assault on the church at the time of the end.

It must be remembered that prophetic Scripture interprets itself when compared with other parallel prophetic Scripture.

Daniel 9:27 teaches that the Antichrist will "cause the sacri-fice to cease." If the Jews are sacrificing, there is a temple. Daniel also revealed that the future Antichrist will set an image in the wing of the Temple (Daniel 12:11); there must be a physical building to set the image of the beast in.

The Temple in Jerusalem had been destroyed for 25 years when the apostle John was told to measure the Temple in Revelation 11:1, 2. According to scholars, John wrote the book of Revelation in A.D. 95! Therefore, John was seeing a temple in Jerusalem during the Tribulation.

John says that the outer court area will be given over to the Gentiles who will then trample the holy city under foot for 42 months (Revelation 11:1-2). I believe the entire conflict during the Tribulation will stem from a Jewish presence be-ing returned to the Temple Mount. Some form of a building for a Jewish presence will be the trigger on the gun that will release the first bullet of the final conflict for Jerusalem.

The fear of the Jews taking possession of the Mount could be seen when Yasser Arafat was in Indonesia. During a press conference, the Palestinian leader flashed a picture I recog-nized as a computer generated photograph printed by the Temple Institute in Jerusalem. The black and white print shows a model of the second Jewish Temple, overlaid on a picture of the Temple Mount. The Dome was removed by com-puter generation and the Jewish Temple had replaced it.

Arafat held the picture up before millions of Muslims in Indonesia, warning of the Jews' desire to remove the Mus-lim mosque and build a Jewish Temple

In the Fall of 2001, Arafat again warned of the desire of the Jews to rebuild the Temple on the Temple Mount. In late 1999, the Islamic Waqf (the revenue agency of mosques in Islamic law) had begun to remove more than 6,000 tons of dirt from underneath an area of the Temple Mount known as Solomon's Stables. The Waqf stated that they desired to make an emergency exit from the underground chamber.

Years ago, I received permission to visit the area located at the southeastern area of the Temple Mount—where the pinnacle of the Temple is located. A large underground room is beneath this area. I was taken aside where a gentleman took an iron bar and hit the floor. It was hollow. He said, "There are many secret chambers underground. We do not know what is underneath this floor."

Muslims granted permission for the entire area to be cleared. It was reported that they want to place an underground mosque in the area. The tons of debris removed erased every trace of Hebrew history in that area. This work may have produced a bulge in the southern wall of the Temple Mount. *The Jerusalem Report* recently issued a press release:

> On 27th August 2002, the archaeologists of the Israeli Antiquities Authority warned that the southern wall of the Temple Mount is in great imminent danger of collapsing. They stated that the bulge in the wall, which was first noticed after Tisha bâAv (the fast commemorating the first two Temples) last year immediately after the Temple Mount Faithful had carried the cornerstone for the Third Temple to the area in front of the southern wall of the Temple Mount, has become much larger. Last year the bulge was 70 cm (29") and was 30 metres (99') long. The bulge has now increased to over 1 metre (39") and is much longer.

Israel's Antiquity Authority is not permitted to go inside and examine the bulge. Should any earthquake movement cause the wall to collapse, Israel will be blamed for the problem, though they had nothing to do with it. The clearing out of the underground chambers for an underground mosque and the Islamic fears that a future Jewish Temple will be erected are causing a flurry of activity at the most controversial property on earth.

Holy Cow, Holy War

The controversy continues with the birth of a red heifer. No one would believe that the birth of a red cow could cause a holy war. According to Torah teaching (Numbers 19), in the time of Moses a pure red heifer was burnt and its ashes were gathered in a clean place. These ashes were mingled with water, symbolically becoming a "water of separation" for the purification of the unclean (v. 9).

Some Jewish sources teach that seven and perhaps 10 red heifers were sacrificed in Israel's history. These ashes were used to purify a person who was ceremonially unclean after touching a dead carcass. Hebrew researchers say that the ashes of a red heifer are needed to eventually purify the sacred furniture in any form of a future Jewish Temple. Several organizations and individuals in Israel have been involved for years in researching this subject and looking for a perfect, kosher red heifer.

Several years ago I visited a farm in the Valley of Megiddo where a red heifer was selected as a candidate for the sacrifice. The cow was guarded because of threats from local Arabs. Later, she turned out to be invalid because portions of her red tail turned white. In the Spring of 2002, another red heifer was born. Several rabbis, including Chaim Richmond, declared the red cow kosher and a possible candidate for an offering.

The idea of a small group of Jews seeking out a red heifer to fulfill a requirement in the Torah, and the fact that another group, the Temple Institute, has researched, designed and crafted items that can be used in a future Jewish Temple agitates nerves in the Islamic world. Perhaps this is why the Palestinian Authority has been working with Saudi leadership, making elaborate and clandestine plans to build the world's largest mosque in Jerusalem on the Temple Mount! They feel a sense of destiny as God prepares the world for the rule of their Mahdi.

WORLD'S LARGEST MOSQUE IN JERUSALEM?

According to an article that appeared in *Israel Today* magazine, the Islamic world has an interest in building the world's largest mosque on the Temple Mount in Jerusalem. Most Muslims do not believe that the two Jewish Temples, built by Solomon and rebuilt after the Babylonian captivity, ever sat on the Temple Mount. In fact, Yasser Arafat stated the Jewish Temple once existed in Nablus. (He is probably alluding to the temple Jesus referred to in John 4:20, 21, that the Samaritans built on Mount Gerizim.)

Islamic spiritual leader Ekrima Sabri, the Arafat-appointed Mufti of Jerusalem and Palestine, announced that the Palestinian Authority is drawing up plans for a new mosque, larger than the one in Mecca, to be built on the Dome of the Rock in Jerusalem. According to Islamic tradition, Mohammed ascended to heaven on his horse from the stone inside the Dome of the Rock, therefore Jerusalem's Temple Mount is the third holiest site to the Islamic religion.

The German newspaper *Die Welt* quoted Sabril in an interview about the history of the Temple Mount:

> There is not the slightest proof that there ever has been a Jewish Temple on the mount. Not a single stone in the whole city of Jerusalem points to any evidence of Jewish history, not even the Western Wall. The only things that archaeologists have been able to find are the remains of buildings from the Arab and Muslim times. The Jews have no valid claim on the Western Wall or the Temple Mount, neither from a religious nor a historical standpoint.

The mufti is either ignorant of archeology or willfully attempting to brainwash less informed people into believing the Jews never had control of Jerusalem in its past. Not only has evidence of a Jewish presence been unearthed in and around Jerusalem, but on the western section of the wall, a large stone dating to the third century A.D. was discovered with old Hebrew writing, "When you shall see this your bones shall rejoice."

A stone fragment with Hebrew writing was discovered in the excavation rubble that said, "To the place of trumpeting."

According to archeologists, it was on the top corner of the wall at the location where the shofar was sounded. This unique discovery was uncovered in ruins that dated back to the destruction of Jerusalem by the Romans in A.D. 70.

Taken But Given Back

During the Six-Day War, Israeli troops captured East Jerusalem from the Jordanians. On the third day, at 10 o'clock in the morning, Jewish soldiers heard over their radios, "We have the city; we are at the Western Wall!"

General Moshe Dayan had the keys to the Temple Mount and could have handed them to the Israeli government. Instead, for fear of causing a major war in the Islamic world, he gave the keys back to the mufti of Jerusalem.

Dr. Asher Kauffman, noted professor at Jerusalem's Hebrew University, was able to walk the Temple Mount and take pictures and measurements prior to its being turned over to the Muslims. He found visible evidence of the Jewish Temple on the Mount itself.

A few years later, these stones and other important objects were removed from the Mount in an attempt to destroy any and all evidence of a Jewish Temple (Source: *Biblical Archeology Review*).

The possibility that the Jews may one day attempt to take control of the Mount is of utmost concern to the Palestinian Authority. They are aware that many Evangelical Christians believe a Jewish Temple will be built in the future. They are also well informed about several organizations, such as the Temple Mount Faithful and the Temple Institute, that are heavily involved in researching and planning a future Temple.

This is one of several reasons the Middle East Muslims are making plans to build the largest mosque in the world on the Temple Mount.

OPENING THE EASTERN GATE

My reliable sources indicate there have been discussions among key Islamic leaders about moving some of the graves in front of the Eastern Gate in Jerusalem, along with the stones that now seal up the gate. A ramp would then be built, enabling worshipers to enter the Temple Mount from the east. This idea was on the drawing board before the 1967 war.

King Hussein of Jordan planned to open the eastern gate to allow Muslims coming from Jordan to enter through the eastern entrance to the Mount. Cranes were being prepared to remove the large blocks when the 1967 war broke out and East Jerusalem, then ruled by the country of Jordan, came under the control of Israel.

It seems the idea for opening the eastern gate is twofold. First, it would give access to the Dome of the Rock and the El Aqsa Mosque from the east. The second reason involves an ancient prophecy from the Bible. The prophet Ezekiel says the gate facing the east will be closed and is for the prince who will come and enter in through the gate (see Ezekiel 44:1-3). If the gate is opened, it would "prove" the Ezekiel prophecy incorrect, thus demonstrating that the Christian and Jewish Scriptures are not true.

Much activity is taking place in and around the Temple Mount area. As modern scholars noted that the Scriptures predict a Jewish presence or Temple in Jerusalem, they struggle to answer the question, "How can a Jewish Temple be constructed on the Temple Mount with an Islamic mosque in the center of the Mount?"

THREE TOUGH QUESTIONS

The very thought of a Jewish presence on the Temple Mount raises three tough questions:

1. Who will actually build a Temple on the Temple Mount?

2. What will happen to the Dome of the Rock when this Temple is built?

3. How would Muslims throughout the world permit anyone to build a Temple near the Dome of the Rock?

These three questions have birthed some wild specula-tion and, sometimes, some not-so-Biblical answers that have been accepted as fact in the Western Christian community. For many years I have heard the theory that a religious Jew must physically rebuild the Temple, because only a Jew would be permitted to rebuild a Temple. This theory is incorrect because Solomon's Temple was built by Gentiles, and Herod, who added onto the second Temple, used Gentiles to help do the physical labor.

This theory has led to the teaching that if the future Antichrist rebuilds the Jewish Temple, the Antichrist must be a Jew. There is no indication in the Scripture this is a fact. It is based on the speculation that the Jews will accept the Antichrist as their Messiah, therefore he must be Jew-ish to be a Messiah.

The Antichrist does not control Jerusalem or the Temple Mount during the first 42 months of the Tribulation period. In fact, the Temple is built during the first 42 months because the Antichrist sets his image in a Temple that is already built (see Revelation 13:14, 15). The Antichrist invades the north-ern horn of Africa, then enters Israel; his forces capture half of Jerusalem, bringing it into captivity (Zechariah 14:2). At this point the Antichrist will sit in the Temple as though he is God (2 Thessalonians 2:4). Therefore, someone else has built the Temple on the Temple Mount and the Antichrist invades the city to "liberate" the sacred Islamic shrine from the hands of the "infidels."

Who will build a place of worship and an altar on the Temple Mount? The answer is found in the Book of Revelation, in the same chapter that tells about a future Temple. Two men, identified as the two witnesses in Revelation 11, will assist in building a temporary Jewish place of worship on the Temple Mount. One of these two witnesses will be Elijah the prophet, according to Malachi 4:5 (Elijah was supernaturally translated into heaven in 2 Kings 2). Jesus said that Elijah will "restore all things" (Matthew 17:11).

John, in Revelation 7, speaks of 144,000 Jews who will be sealed with the seal of God during the first part of the 7-year Tribulation. Early Jewish rabbis believed that, when Elijah appears, he will be given the knowledge of which tribe every Jew is originally from.

A dear friend, Mike Coleman, once spoke to Professor Asher Kauffman in Israel about the possibilities of a third Temple being constructed in Jerusalem. Mr. Kaufman told Coleman that if the Jews were to rebuild a Temple, it would take 42 months from the beginning until the time the first sacrifice would be offered at the dedication. The reason? During the rebuilding process, certain prayers would be said and certain purification rituals would transpire during the new moons and feast days.

The strange parallel is that the two witnesses of Revelation 11 will begin and conclude their ministry during a 42-month period (Revelation 11:1-4). At the conclusion of their ministry, the Antichrist will cause the sacrifice to cease. This sacrifice would possibly occur during the actual dedication of the Temple area, slated to occur during a Jewish Passover season.

Muslims will never permit anyone to build a Jewish worship house on the property where an Islamic shrine has sat for 1,300 years. It would incite bloodshed against Jews throughout the world.

Yet, these two witnesses will be given such authority that they will bring death to their enemies through their words! Any attempts to hinder their ministry will be met with swift judgement and instant destruction (see Revelation 11:5).

This will cause fear in all people, including Muslims. Supernatural power will form a hedge of protection for the witnesses during the first 42 months of the 7-year Tribulation.

WHAT ABOUT THE DOME OF THE ROCK?

If a Jewish Temple sits on the Temple Mount, what will happen to the Dome of the Rock? Will the two coexist, or will the Dome be removed? The answer to this question stems from understanding where the true location of the ancient Holy of Holies from the previous Jewish Temples are located.

Some place the Holy of Holies to the north of the Dome of the Rock.Others have recently given evidence that the Ark of the Covenant once sat on the "foundation stone," the large rock located in the center of the mosque called the Dome of the Rock.

Some have speculated that a Jewish Temple could not be built unless the Mosque was removed. This has sparked some rather bizarre theories. One theory teaches that a massive earthquake will take the Dome down, thus clearing the path for the Jewish Temple. Another theory, represented in Christian movies, is that the Dome will be physically removed by a missile attack during a major conflict. Another theory circulating says that the Jews could pay a huge amount of money to have the Dome moved to Arabia. I personally do not agree with these three theories.

1. *The Earthquake Theory.* The Dome has been damaged several times by earthquakes and repaired. The fact is that after an earthquake, the Dome would simply be repaired.

2. *The Missile Attack.* An attack against this Islamic holy site would cause a war unlike any the Middle East has ever seen. More than a billion Muslims would go to war to defend their holy sites. Any pre-planned damage to any mosque would only bring retaliation and eventual repairs.

3. *Moving the Mosque.* This theory is too ridiculous to spend time answering. No Muslim would remove the mosque from the Temple Mount, and anyone who would plan such a mission would not live to see the sunrise.

THE FOURTH THEORY

The fourth and most plausible theory is that the Dome will remain intact, and the Jewish Temple will be rebuilt in another location on the Mount. In John's vision in the Book of Revelation, he was told to measure the Temple but omit the outer court because it would be given to the Gentiles (Revelation 11:2). If a Jewish Temple were built to the north of the Dome, the outer court would be the place where the Dome is sitting.

After examining this theory, I once took a group to the top of the Temple Mount, and we began to step off the size of the Holy Place from Christ's time. The guards watched us and suspected what we were doing; but before we were literally removed from the Mount, we concluded that several hundred feet exists from the north of the Dome to the outside Mosque wall.

Sources have informed me that in the past, peace discussions suggested dividing the Temple Mount into three parts: one for the Muslims, one for the Jews and another for Christians. Pope John Paul, especially, has secretly propagated this idea. This could work because Muslims worship on Friday, the Jews on Saturday, and the Christians on Sunday.

Prior to President Clinton's leaving office, he suggested that since the Jewish people were giving up large amounts of land, in the name of peace, the Muslims should allow the Jews a portion of the Temple Mount for a place of worship. Needless to say, this was completely rejected by Yasser Arafat.

If the Temple Mount is the heart of the problem, then Jerusalem is the blood that feeds the heart. In fact, Jerusalem is said to be the heart of the earth and the center of the nations. This may be true in more than just a spiritual sense.

Eight

MEGIDDO: BATTLE AT THE GATES

And he gathered them together into a place called in the
Hebrew tongue Armageddon (Revelation 16:16).

Since America and other democratic nations around
the globe have declared war on terrorism, common people
on the street with little knowledge of the Bible have used
the word "Armageddon" to describe the battle we are in.
Armageddon is not just a Biblical or prophetic word, it is a
geographical location in Israel where the final conflict of
the nations will climax with the physical return of Jesus
(see Revelation 19).

Prior to this final confrontation, there will be a series
of wars in the region of the Middle East. One such conflict
is recorded in Ezekiel 38 and 39. This attack is designed
to destroy Israel, and the nations involved are presently
Islamic countries. They include:

- ◆ Persia (Iran) – Ezekiel 38:5
- ◆ Ethiopia – Ezekiel 38:5
- ◆ Libya – Ezekiel 38:5
- ◆ Gomer (Armenia) – Ezekiel 38:6
- ◆ Togarmah (portions of Turkey) – Ezekiel 38:6
- ◆ Gog and Magog (former southern Soviet states) – Ezekiel 38:2, 3

The prophet gave detailed information relating to the conditions in Israel prior to the invasion.

> Gomer, and all his bands; the house of Togarmah of the north quarters, and all his bands: and many people with thee (Ezekiel 38:6).

The phrase "house of Togarmah" is unique. Togarmah was the son of Gomer who was the son of Japheth, and the grandson of Noah (see Genesis 10:1-3). According to the *International Standard Bible Encyclopedia*, Togarmah is probably present day Armenia. In Ezekiel's time it was a tribal region northeast of Asia Minor. Today it would include the areas of Armenia and parts of the soviet country of Georgia. Togarmah is referred to with "bands" of people within. This nation forms a confederation of Islamic nations to attack Israel from several directions.

Matthew Henry, in his commentary notes on Ezekiel 38, points out that the Syrian general, Antiochus, who invaded Jerusalem and defiled the Temple, had a coalition consisting of the nations mentioned in this passage. Yet, there is no indication that this prophecy was fulfilled at that time. Ezekiel gives the timing of this battle:

WHEN ISRAEL RETURNS TO THE LAND BROUGHT BACK FROM THE SWORD

After many days thou shalt be visited: in the latter years thou shalt come into the land that is brought back from

Empires of Prophecy from Daniel Chapter Two
The Vision of the Metallic Image

The Head of Gold:
Babylonian Empire
606 BC to 536 BC

The Chest and Arms of Silver:
Medes and Persians
536 BC to 336 BC

The Thighs of Brass:
Grecian Empire
336 BC to 63 BC

The Legs of Iron:
Roman Empire
63 BC to 476 AD

The Holy Roman Empire divided between east (Constantinople) and west (Rome). 11th Century AD

Legs of Iron and Clay
Communism or Democracy, or Christianity (clay) and Islam (iron)

Ten Toes of Iron and Clay
Ten final kings—five from the Roman Empire and five from Constantinople

The Four Major Empires of Prophecy

THE BABYLONIAN EMPIRE
about 600 B.C.

THE PERSIAN EMPIRE
about 450 B.C.

THE GREEK EMPIRE
about 300 B.C.

THE ROMAN EMPIRE
in the time of Christ

Archaeological Evidence
of an Ancient Jewish Presence in Israel

This excavation at the Western wall in Jerusalem
unearthed evidence of Jerusalem's destruction in 70 AD.

Buried for 17 centuries, this stone has Hebrew writing that quotes a verse from Isaiah:
"When you see this, your bones shall rejoice."

Discovered in an excavation, this Jewish menorah (candlestick)
was carved into a stone in a large ancient walkway.

Workers on Mount Gerizim discovered twelve large stones (possibly an altar)
and one large stone with old Hebrew writing, believed to be from Joshua's time
(see Joshua 24:26-27).

Archaeologists in the West Bank unearthed the ancient ruins of the temple on Mount Gerizim, built for the Samaritans by Sanballat in the time of Nehemiah.

The ancient temple of the Samaritans is where Yasser Arafat claimed the real Jewish temple used to be. According to the Palestinians, the Temple Mount in Jerusalem is 100% Muslim.

The Battle for Jerusalem

1967—Israeli troops overlook the Temple Mount,
moments before breaking through the Lion's Gate into the city.

1967—General Moshe Dayan gave the keys to the Temple Mount
back to Muslim authorities to help keep peace.

1967—On the third day of the Six Day War,
Rabbi Goren blows the shofar at the Western Wall in Jerusalem.

1967—Troops rejoice and people spent days at the Western Wall praying and celebrating.

Russian Jews returning en masse back to Israel (see Jeremiah 16:14-16)

Muslims have built a new entrance underground, into Solomon's Stables.
It is a large underground mosque.

Former CIA agent Bill Hall (far left),
who warned my father in the 1970's about Islamic fanatics using planes.

This mosque in Karbala, Iraq contains a gold and silver decorated shrine to Imam Hussein,
the grandson of Mohammed. Many Shiite Muslims believe the Mahdi will emerge from Karbala.

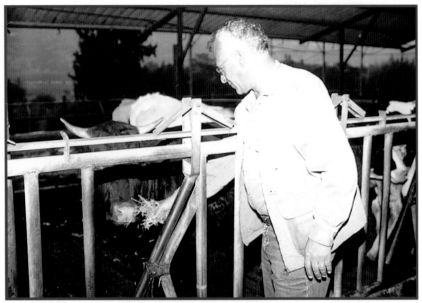

The birth of this red heifer caused quite a stir among some Jewish and Muslim groups.

The Dome of the Rock mosque was built over this stone,
where some believe the Jewish Temple once existed.

A full lunar eclipse is considered a "blood moon." (See Acts 2:19-20)

In Uzbekistan, this lamb was born with two marks.
One resembles the word for "Mohammed" and the other "Allah" in Arabic.

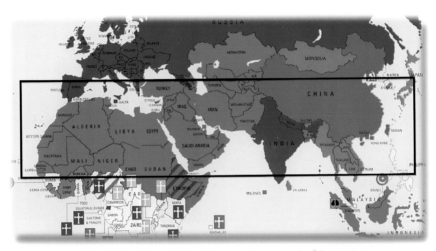

The 10/40 window stretches from ten degrees north of the equator
to forty degrees latitude north of the equator, and extends from northwest Africa to East Asia.
It is where 95% of the population has never heard the gospel.
Iraq is in the heart of the 10/40 window.

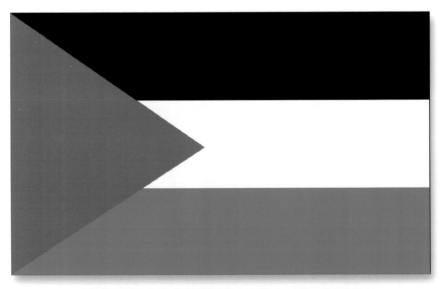

The four colors in the Palestinian flag are black, white, red and green.
These colors are also identified on the four horses of the apocalypse in Revelation 6:1-8.
The Greek word for "pale" in Revelation 6:8 is *chloros*, translated as "green" in the Bible.

the sword, and is gathered out of many people, against the mountains of Israel, which have been always waste: but it is brought forth out of the nations, and they shall dwell safely all of them (Ezekiel 38:8).

The Jews were dispersed twice. In 606 B.C., Jerusalem and the Temple were destroyed by Nebuchadnezzar. It was destroyed the second time in 70 A.D. by the Romans, who burned the Temple and the city, and took the Jews captive. After the death of six million Jews at the hands of the Nazis, God brought the Jewish people back to their original homeland. Although terrorist attacks bring fear to many, Israel has a strong military force and today, the Jews have returned from their captivity.

WHEN ISRAEL DWELLS IN SAFETY

And thou shalt say, I will go up to the land of unwalled villages; I will go to them that are at rest, that dwell safely, all of them dwelling without walls, and having neither bars nor gates (v. 11).

Four times Ezekiel refers to Israel dwelling safely (vv. 8, 11, 14; 39:26). The word *safely* can also allude to security. Some would contend that Israel is not dwelling safely since she is surrounded by aggressive Muslim neighbors who seek her destruction, and is exposed to the blasts of suicide bombers. After visiting Israel 21 times, I have visited most areas in daylight and at night without any fear or intimidation.

WHEN ISRAEL DWELLS IN UNWALLED VILLAGES

And thou shalt say, I will go up to the land of unwalled villages; I will go to them that are at rest, that dwell safely, all of them dwelling without walls, and having neither bars nor gates (Ezekiel 38:11).

In Ezekiel's time, the cities of Israel were built on high mountains and hills. They were surrounded by large stone walls and watchtowers. One example is the *tel* (hill) of Megiddo located in the Jezreel valley. In Ahab and Solomon's time, this fortified stronghold was a city surrounded by huge hand-cut, limestone rocks with large gates and guard towers.

Today, no modern Israeli city has a protective wall surrounding it. The unwalled villages will be a target to the invading armies during the coming war.

WHEN DESLOATE PLACES ARE INHABITED

> To take a spoil, and to take a prey; to turn thine hand upon the desolate places that are now inhabited, and upon the people that are gathered out of the nations, which have gotten cattle and goods, that dwell in the midst of the land (Ezekiel 38:12).

Since 1985, I have traveled to Israel and observed where deserts have been transformed into farms, and where once-empty places are now inhabited. One of the major signs of the coming of the Messiah is that the wilderness and the desert will blossom and produce fruit (see Isaiah 35:1). The produce in Israel can not only feed the entire nation of Israel, but tons of produce is shipped throughout the world. This was predicted 2,800 years ago by Isaiah the prophet:

> He shall cause them that come of Jacob to take root: Israel shall blossom and bud, and fill the face of the world with fruit (Isaiah 27:6).

WHEN THE LATTER YEARS ARRIVE

Ezekiel emphasizes that this battle will ensue in the latter years.

> After many days thou shalt be visited: in the latter years thou shalt come into the land that is brought back from the sword (Ezekiel 38:8).

And thou shalt come up against my people of Israel, as a cloud to cover the land; it shall be in the latter days, and I will bring thee against my land, that the heathen may know me, when I shall be sanctified in thee, O Gog, before their eyes (Ezekiel 38:16).

The word latter used in these Scriptures means "the last," "the end" or "the future." Generally, the whole phrase is used by Old Testament prophets to indicate the time frame on earth prior to the final great battle and the return of the Lord to the earth. The phrase *latter days* is used 11 times in the Scripture. The words *last days* are recorded eight times in the Bible. In the New Testament, the phrase is connected to the time prior to the return of the Lord (see James 5:3; 2 Peter 3:3).

In summary, this Scripture makes it clear that the battle, called the war with Gog and Magog, will occur in the future. Several important features mark this battle:

THE LAND WILL BE POLLUTED FOR SEVEN MONTHS

And they shall sever out men of continual employment, passing through the land to bury with the passengers those that remain upon the face of the earth, to cleanse it: after the end of seven months shall they search (Ezekiel 39:14).

Why would anyone wait seven months before searching for the remains of those slain in battle? I believe this could be a clue revealing that chemical or biological weapons may be used in this battle. Nations such as Iran and Iraq have been working on developing weapons of mass destruction, including chemical, biological and even nuclear weapons.

With the fall of the Soviet Union, several of the southern Russian nations are Muslim and have in their possession weapons that have been stolen or purchased and sold to radical Islamic nations. The weapons in the former Soviet

Union are often traded in return for hard cash and, in some cases, drugs. The drugs are given to the contact person who, in return, brings across the border the weapons or the technology. The drugs are sold in Russia on the black market and the weapons or technology are placed in the arsenal of dangerous men.

Fire, Brimstone and Hail Accompany the Battle

And I will plead against him with pestilence and with blood; and I will rain upon him, and upon his bands, and upon the many people that are with him, an overflowing rain, and great hailstones, fire, and brimstone (38:22).

The word *brimstone* alludes to sulfur. In ancient times the weapons of war were swords, spears and chariots. Now the weapons contain fire and smoke. If certain fiery weapons are used, they could produce forms of radiation. Therefore, the bodies of the dead would lie in the polluted fields for seven months, until strangers are hired to mark the places where the skeletons are lying.

It Will Take Seven Years to Burn the Weapons

And they that dwell in the cities of Israel shall go forth, and shall set on fire and burn the weapons, both the shields and the bucklers, the bows and the arrows, and the handstaves, and the spears, and they shall burn them with fire seven years (v. 9).

This unique verse of prophecy shows that after this battle, it will take Israel seven years to destroy all of the weapons of the enemy. Israel has been involved in five different wars—in 1948, 1956, 1967, 1973 and 1981. Scattered throughout modern Israel are rusty remains of jeeps, tanks and vehicles—silent monuments of past war victories.

In Ezekiel's time, it would take months to destroy weapons made of wood, including bows, arrows and handles of spears. In this future conflict, it will indeed take seven years to destroy and burn the weapons of war.

WHO IS MISSING IN THE LIST OF NATIONS?

It is possible that there will be a war prior to this one. It is interesting to note the nations missing from the Ezekiel list. Egypt, for example, is not mentioned. Egypt has fought Israel in four of the past five wars, and is amassing a huge arsenal; yet, this country is not listed.

Syria fought Israel in four of the past five wars and is pressuring Israel to give back the Golan Heights. Yet, Syria is missing from Ezekiel's mix of nations. This has led scholars to speculate that something has happened in these nations prior to the attack on Israel by their Islamic brothers.

The three theories are: (1) Egypt and Syria have been involved in a war prior to Ezekiel 38, 39 and are in a defeated condition; therefore, they do not join the coalition. (2) Egypt and Syria sit back while the other nations get involved, waiting to see the outcome. This is possible because both Egypt and Syria have suffered great losses in wars against Israel. Years ago, a Syrian pilot defected to Israel and told the Israeli military that no Syrian pilot believed they could ever defeat Israel in a war.

Other nations also sit back and watch the battle without ever getting involved. In fact, it appears that Israel will stand alone at the time this conflict happens. Some have asked, "Where is the United States during this time?" While the United States is not alluded to in the Old Testament prophecies, there are some interesting names written in 38:13:

> Sheba, and Dedan, and the merchants of Tarshish, with all the young lions thereof, shall say unto thee, Art thou come to take a spoil? hast thou gathered thy company to take a prey? to carry away silver and gold, to take away cattle and goods, to take a great spoil?

Sheba, Dedan and Tarshish are not involved in the attack, but are asking a question to the armies invading Israel. Tracing these names through the Bible, it appears Sheba is the Arabians, or more specifically, those in the area of Saudi Arabia.

Dedan would be in the area of the country of Jordan. In Ezekiel's day the merchants of Tarshish were from Tyre and Sidon, cities in present day Lebanon. It is uncertain whom "all the young lions" refer to, although some have concluded that this is alluding to the British Isles.

ISRAEL WILL STAND ALONE

Israel will win this conflict and defeat many of the surrounding Arab and Islamic nations. In the light of recent events, there may be three reasons why America is not directly involved with this conflict:

1. America is involved in her own military conflict
2. America has been worn down both economically and militarily
3. America has turned away from Israel

Within days of the terrorist attack on America, airlines were talking about laying off up to 150,000 people. Hotels were half-filled and popular tourist attractions were pulling in a fraction of their normal traffic. Over 3,000 souls went into eternity, unexpectedly, on September 11, 2001.

America entered a military conflict against an enemy that is like a spider in a rain forest. With hundreds of terrorist cells and thousands of Islamic terrorists in the world, America may see a conflict similar to what Israel has experienced in the Middle East. While we may eventually be secure in our own borders, Americans and Christians living outside of the Western Hemisphere will be walking targets, especially in nations that permit extreme Islamic fundamentalism.

It is clear that the aftermath of terrorism does more damage than the attack itself. The fear, depression and economic woes that follow a major assault inflict a greater national burden than a war fought on foreign soil. America could stretch out her troops around the world and not be present when the northern bear meets the lions of Judah on the mountains of Israel (Ezekiel 39:2).

With America's strong Christian base, many understand the prophetic importance of Israel. During the Clinton administration, political talking heads would often chirp that America should change her policy toward our greatest friend in the Middle East, Israel. Even today, we hear our public officials say that Israel should give up land that was gained in previous wars in exchange for peace.

But we ought to look in our own back yard. Did America steal Texas and New Mexico from the Mexicans during a war? Should we sign it back over to Mexico? Did our early fathers leave a trail of blood and tears as they forced the Indians westward? If so, should we return the land of their ancestors? When wars are fought, boundaries change. Every modern nation in Europe once had a different boundary, yet no European is demanding that they go back to the boundaries of the Grecian or Roman Empires!

The Bible indicates that God gave the land to Abraham and his children, through Isaac, and by a blood covenant:

> And he said unto him, I am the Lord that brought thee out
> of Ur of the Chaldees, to give thee this land to inherit it
> (Genesis 15:7).

In 1948, 1956, 1967 and 1973, the enemies of Israel rose up in war to destroy the Jewish state. In 1973, a surprise attack by Syria could have destroyed the nation. Yet, Israel prevailed despite incredible odds. Yes, there was land that was taken during these wars. In the eyes of Israel, the enemy attacked and Israel won; therefore, as the adage says, "All is fair in love and war." Yet, in the eyes of the Palestinians and especially the Muslims, Israel is holding property that does not belong to them. Therefore, some terrorize the Jews hoping they will leave the land. The term "land for peace" implies that "if we don't get land then Israel will have terrorism."

Herein lies the conflict that baffles the West. "Why not give up some dirt and piles of rocks if it would ensure the safety of the Jewish State?" some ask. Because Israeli leaders know something about fanatical Islam that the West is only now learning. A terrorist is not interested in negotiating with his enemies; he is interested in the elimination of his enemies.

TERRORISM: THE FINAL WEAPON OF MASS DESTRUCTION

Terrorism will be the leading weapon that paves the path to Armageddon. The future Antichrist and his armies will hold nations hostage with modern weapons of fear and death. Revelation 17 paints a picture of Mystery Babylon, a cryptic name used in John's time for Rome. The prophetic vision reveals that "the great city ruling over the kings of the earth will be destroyed in one hour" (Revelation 17:18; 18:10).

Over 1,900 years ago, Rome was built with stone blocks. Destruction in one hour was impossible then. In our age, nuclear weapons can destroy an entire city in moments. They produce a mushroom cloud filled with radiation. Revelation says men will stand afar off for fear of the smoke (see 18:10-15). The 10 kings of Bible prophecy will burn the city with fire (17:16). Prior to the visible return of Christ, mankind will be so filled with hatred that unless God shortens the days, no one will remain alive on the planet.

> Unless those days were shortened, no flesh would be saved . . .
> for the elect's sake those days will be shortened (Matthew 24:22).

In the Western mind we think, *How could mankind be that cruel, to kill one another to the point of extinction?* The answer is Islamic jihad. Ask a Muslim what jihad means and you will receive several different answers. It took terror for Americans to familiarize themselves with the word. It refers to an Islamic holy war. To a terrorist, Islamic Jihad is a war against the West, against the Jews and against the Christians.

A fanatical terrorist believes that if he dies a martyr in a jihad, his death grants him the honor of going to paradise where he will sit with the greatest Islamic scholars of all times, including the prophet himself. He will be attended, he believes, by 72 virgins.

As America pursues this new war, I believe many Americans will demand a change in how we look at Israel, based on the false notion that we can stop the terrorism in our nation if we change our political opinions about Israel. This was Arafat's deal—give up the land and get peace. The dove of peace flew over the White House in 1993, flew to Israel, then flew away! Terrorism is not stopped by negotiations.

Muslim clerics living in Israel are speaking with a double mouth. While smiling for the cameras and sincerely stating their hearts' burning desire for land and for peace, behind the curtain and in their mosques they are saying they will get the land . . . then more land . . . then all of the land . . . and eventually kill the Jews. It is a part of their teaching that the Jews must be killed!

A NUCLEAR HOSTAGE

The more moderate and secular Muslims are turned off by the fanatic, and some I know in the Middle East get along quite well with Christians and Jews. They teach that Mohammed was dealing with the culture of his time and Muslims must adjust to the time. This enrages the fanatics. In the future, terrorism will take on a new dimension:

Airports will be secure and hijacking an airliner will look like an ancient maneuver from a bygone era. The 21st century terrorist activities could entail:

- hacking into computers and shutting down businesses and large corporations,

- bringing biological and chemical substances into a city, or by killing thousands at a time by placing a nuclear bomb in a briefcase and detonating it over a major city, or

- using electronically guided weapons that can knock a plane from the sky.

We are not many years away from all of this happening. But before the great battles of prophecy, there will be a time of false peace that will lull the world into a false sense of security. The Antichrist will be at the forefront in announcing this new season of peace among the nations.

Yet, hidden deep within his heart is the desire to fulfill the ancient predictions of Islam—that one day the Jews will be destroyed and Islam will rule the world.

Nine

WHEN ISLAM RULES THE WORLD

All those (who believe in the Bible) are two-faced and traitorous. There is no hope of amending the traits, morals and behavior of Bible believers, as long as they cling to what is written in their Bible. The only solution for dealing with this (Bible) ideology is its liquidation (May, 1, 1986 and February 1, 1988 issues of *A-Riyad*, the official newspaper of the Saudi Royal Court).

Who is like unto the beast? who is able to make war with him? And there was given unto him a mouth speaking great things and blasphemies; and power was given unto him to continue forty and two months. And he opened his mouth in blasphemy against God, to blaspheme his name, and his tabernacle, and them that dwell in heaven.

And it was given unto him to make war with the saints, and to overcome them: and power was given him over all kindreds, and tongues, and nations (Revelation 13:4-7).

The Assignment Has Begun

Fifty years ago, the very thought that a militant Islamic leader could unite a radical Islamic coalition into a feared global threat would have been considered fiction. Twenty-five years ago the possibility of a violent Middle Eastern dictator gaining access to weapons of mass destruction was discussed among military brass only behind closed doors. Today, the threat is not *if* this possibility exists, but *when* the moment of attack will come.

As you have discovered, the Islamic religion has an agenda. This agenda is both practical and prophetic. The practical plan is to expand the Islamic crescent from its Middle East stronghold into Europe and Asia, and to eventually dominate the large cities in North America. The prophetic agenda is to ensure that the predictions and traditions of its founder, Mohammad, are fulfilled. In Mohammad's day the Islamic religion grew by the use of the sword, and forced conversion.

Today, it grows through large Muslim families, conversion and, in some countries, forced conversion. Despite the smooth tongue of well-educated Muslims telling the West not to worry, the sword of fanatical Islam is once again slashing its way through nations, slaying the "infidels" who would resist conversion to the religion of Allah. As the Koran says:

> The punishment of those who wage war against Allah and his Apostle, and strive with might and main for mischief through the land is: execution, or crucifixion, or the cutting off of the hands and feet from from opposite sides or exile from the land (Surah V.36).

It was once thought impossible that small, Third World nations would ever become a threat to modern existence. After all, America and Russia were the two super powers possessing weapons that create mushroom clouds. After the fall of Communism, the Soviet Union became a black marketer's dream. Weapons were sold for drugs and much needed money. In the early 90's one source informed me that the Iraqi government had hired over 500 former Soviet Union scientists working on its weapons program. These included several men knowledgeable in nuclear weapons development. But it is not just Iraq; Syria, Iran and Libya are all interested in amassing this dangerous arsenal of death. The campaign to arm fanatics and bring jihad to the shores of the West has now begun.

HOSTAGE TO THE WEAPONS

Imagine this scenario: A Middle Eastern diplomat working at the United Nations has secretly arranged to have certain packages delivered into the United States via a foreign ship. The individual packages are as small as a briefcase. On their arrival, a contact intercepts the packages and delivers them to the "proper" sources. Within a few months, a small nuclear bomb has been built and hidden in Brooklyn, New York.

On the west coast another "cell agent" has arranged for a series of packages to arrive via ship to a specific location. This package holds five sealed vials of a deadly biological plague. The vials are secured at an undisclosed location, until a coded signal is given.

A third "cell leader" effectively crosses the Mexican border into Texas. He too is carrying a special chemical, called X-1. It is a nerve agent that can be released in the air without being detected. The deadly chemical is placed in a secure room in an apartment building, shared by two men who are part of the "sleeper cells" Americans have been warned about for months.

On a pre-determined signal, the head of an Islamic coalition from the Middle East contacts the United States

President demanding he pressure the Israelis to pull out of the Palestinian territories and East Jerusalem once and for all. They demand that in 30 days, Israel release to the international community all their nuclear weapons. If the American government and Israel fail to respond within 30 days, the nuclear bomb will be released in the largest Jewish community in the world, Brooklyn, New York. The biological agents will be spread across Los Angeles and Houston, Texas. Because the secret agents were careful to conceal their arsenal, no one in the federal or state government knows where the dangerous bomb and the frightening chemical substances are hidden.

Suddenly, America is held hostage by an invisible threat.The fear factor strikes the heart of America as the media discusses on the evening news the possibilities of millions of deaths resulting from this possible attack. What does the President do? If he says "no," then he will be blamed for millions of deaths. What do you think the average American would do? I believe they would force Israel to do what the terrorists have demanded. After all, they reason, why should Americans suffer for what a group of Jews are doing 10,000 miles away in another country?

The above picture is not impossible. In fact, it is quite probable in the future. Islam wants Jerusalem, Israel and death to the Jews. This may be why the Biblical prophet, Zechariah, said that "Jerusalem would become a cup of trembling to all nations" (Zechariah 12:2). The prophet also predicted that Jerusalem would become a "burdensome stone to all the nations round about" (Zechariah 12:3). This verse infers that dealing with Jerusalem will be like carrying a huge, very heavy stone on one's shoulders.

As stated earlier, Jerusalem is the center of the world's three monotheistic religions: Christianity, Islam and Judaism. The Temple Mount is holy to the Christians, because Christ was crucified near Mount Moriah. It is holy to the Jews because both Temples once stood proudly on the mountain, it is holy to Muslims because two mosques now rest on the hill. Because the old city of Jerusalem, and East Jerusalem are surrounded by Jews and Christian churches, fanatical Muslims believe the "infidel" Jews and Christians must be expelled to purify this, the third most sacred site to Islam.

All methods of expulsion have failed and will continue to do so until the intrusion of the Antichrist. He and his people will successfully "liberate" Jerusalem from the "infidels." His success will be his ability to merge a coalition, and successfully hold nations hostage with his spectacular arsenal of weapons.

THE ANTICHRIST AND HIS WEAPONS

In Revelation 13, John announces the appearance of the Beast and his kingdom. John asks, "Who can make war against the beast?" (Revelation 13:4). Later in the same prophetic book, we read where the beast and his 10 kings destroy a large city in an hour (Revelation 18:10, 17, 19).

This powerful blast produces a "smoke" that creates fear in the hearts of those standing afar off, observing the destruction (Revelation 18:9, 18). Within an hour, these 10 kings will "give their kingdoms (nations) over to the beast" (Revelation 17:12). After carefully researching the chapters alluding to these passages, I believe the reason nations submit to the Beast is the fear that he will destroy both the leaders and people in any country that resist him. This is how Saddam was successful in retaining power in Iraq. He murdered thousands of his own people, the Kurds, including anyone who disagreed with his mode of operation.

The Biblical prophets visualized many wars prior to the return of the Messiah. During these battles, men would die in a manner unknown to the prophet. Imagine when

Zechariah saw the vision of the final battle for Jerusalem and how men would die:

> And this shall be the plague wherewith the Lord will smite all the people that have fought against Jerusalem; their flesh shall consume away while they stand upon their feet, and their eyes shall consume away in their holes, and their tongue shall consume away in their mouth (Zechariah 14:12).

This prophecy alludes to the time when the armies of the Antichrist surround Jerusalem. Some say the flesh of men melting alludes to the moment that Christ returns and, by the brightness of His coming, destroys the global armies, thus eliminating those who would attempt to eliminate the Jews (see 2 Thessalonians 1:1-10).

Others believe it reveals a weapon of unbelievable power that literally melts the human flesh while the person is still standing on their feet. Such weapons, nonexistent in Zechariah's day, are now locked in silos on military bases!

China, North Korea and Russia are actively selling ballistic missiles to Middle Eastern nations. The real danger is not a ballistic missile, but a missile warhead tipped with biological and chemical weapons.

After the Gulf War, United Nations inspectors entered Iraq and were shocked to discover 50 chemical-filled ballistic warheads, 12,694 mustard gas-filled artillery shells and over 10,000 sarin-filled artillery shells and rocket warheads. They also discovered 300 tons of bulk agent ready for use (*Source*: Hal Lindsey, *The Final Battle*, p. 187). And Saddam claimed he had no "weapons of mass destruction!"

The future Beast will use his own stash of weapons to institute his own form of justice on surrounding nations. No one will be successful in conquering him or stopping his progress of taking possession of nations. This is why Daniel identified this Beast as "dreadful and terrible" (Daniel 7:19). Daniel said this man would use peace to destroy many.

> Through his policy also he shall cause craft to prosper in his
> hand; and he shall magnify himself in his heart, and by peace
> shall destroy many: he shall also stand up against the Prince
> of princes; but he shall be broken without hand (Daniel 8:25).

How could people be destroyed through peace? The word *craft* means "deceit and fraud". Daniel is saying that through the Antichrist's knowledge, he will be successful with deceit and fraud. This deceit will be linked to his so-called peace agreements that will eventually be broken. A passage in Daniel 11:27, paints a picture of his deception while negotiating:

> And both these kings' hearts shall be to do mischief, and
> they shall speak lies at one table; but it shall not prosper:
> for yet the end shall be at the time appointed (Daniel 11:27).

A seven-year covenant (in Daniel 9:27, the Hebrew word for week is a period of seven years), will be signed with many nations. In the middle of the seven years, the coming Beast will break the treaty and set up an abomination (an image of the beast) in Jerusalem:

> And he shall make a strong covenant with many for one
> week; and for half of the week he shall cause sacrifice and
> offering to cease; and upon the wing of abominations shall
> come one who makes desolate, until the decreed end is
> poured out on the desolator (Daniel 9:27, *RSV*).

The Antichrist will promise *peace*, yet through *peace* he will destroy many? The word *peace* in this passage is literally "security". He will tell people they will have security if they follow him. How ironic, that the Palestinians use this same theme when negotiating with the Israelis. Israel demands security and the Palestinians promise "land for peace."

Just as the Oslo peace accords collapsed, the future promises of peace signed by Islamic nations with Israel will be a covenant of deceit. The word for *destroy* in this passage means *ruin* or *decay*. This passage could read, "And promising security he will ruin many."

It may seem strange, but certain Muslims are expecting peace treaties to be signed, and the Mahdi will rule for seven years. In the article *Who is Imam Mahdi*, the Islamic writer pointed out (*www.islam.tc/prophecies/imam.html*):

Hadrat Abu Khudri (R.A.) relates that Rasulullah (Sallallahu Alayhi Wasallam) said:

Al Mahdi will be from my progeny. His forehead will be broad and his nose will be high. He will fill the world with justice and fairness at a time when the world will be filled with oppression. He will rule for seven years.

The writer continues:

[A] large number of people from Iraq will come to him and pledge their allegiance to him. This person (Imam Mahdi) will distribute the spoils of war after the battle. He will lead the people according to the Sunnat and during his reign Islam will spread throughout the world. He will remain till seven years (since his emergence). He will pass away.

Another interesting observation is made in the following statement:

There will be four peace agreements signed between you and the Romans. The fourth agreement will be mediated through a person who will be from the progeny of Hadrat Haroon (A.S.) and will be upheld for seven years.

Three observations are to be made from these Islamic traditions:

1. They believe a peace agreement will be signed and upheld for seven years.

2. The agreements will come after a major war.

3. The Mahdi will rule for seven years, then die.

Now, compare these Islamic traditions with the revelation in the Scriptures:

1. The coming dictator signs a peace treaty for seven years (Daniel 9:27).

2. The treaty will be signed after some major wars in the Middle East.

3. The man who signs the treaty will be destroyed at the end of seven years.

Muslim have not taken their traditions from the Bible, but their expectations of the Mahdi are very akin to the predictions found in the prophetic books of the Scriptures. The common question is, how will surrounding Arab-Muslim nations make peace with Israel, when there is such hatred between these two brothers?

THE TIMING OF A FALSE PEACE

At the present time, most Islamic nations are uninterested in peace with Israel. The majority is supporting the internal uprising between the Palestinians and Israelis, and others are calling for an all out holy war (jihad) against Jews living in "Palestine." If Israel were to defeat surrounding nations in a major war, the international community would demand a peace settlement.

Such a war is coming, as mentioned in chapter eight. During the Gog and Magog conflict, all but a sixth of the enemy armies will be killed. It will be the greatest war victory in Israel's history. Some scholars speculate this would be the time when Syria will be utterly destroyed. The city of Damascus is the oldest continuing city on earth and has never been destroyed in the manner the prophet Isaiah predicted. Isaiah wrote:

> The burden of Damascus. Behold, Damascus is taken away from being a city, and it shall be a ruinous heap. In that day shall his strong cities be as a forsaken bough, and an uppermost branch, which they left because of the children of Israel: and there shall be desolation (Isaiah 17:1, 9).

Since 1948, Israel has fought five wars with its Arab neighbors. Syria has been involved in four of the past five conflicts. If Syria sent a chemical or biological weapon on the Israeli population, Israel would not restrain from utterly destroying the enemy. If Damascus were destroyed, then Baghdad would become the leading city in the old Babylonian crescent, stretching from Lebanon to Syria and Iraq.

After the Gog and Magog war, many believe the seven-year agreement of Daniel 9:27 will be signed. It may be that the Islamic nations will realize that Israel, as a nation, is not going anywhere. They may understand that future wars could mean total annihilation for all humans in the Middle East. Islamic nations will only agree to peace with Israel after a war resulting in many Islamic deaths, has ended.

I'm certain the United Nations will lead the way for a major peace treaty at the beginning of the seven-year Tribulation.This may be what Revelation 6:2 alludes to, where John saw a rider on a white horse. Scripture indicates this white horse rider will receive a crown, and power to conquer. Each time I read this I am reminded that all United Nations (U.N.) vehicles throughout the world are white in color. The United Nations is offering Israel and the Palestinians the opportunity to guard the roads and checkpoints in Israel. At this time, Israel has rejected the offer. The United Nations has power to place economic and military sanctions on entire nations (Iraq is an example).

The white horse rider could symbolically allude to the power of a U.N. leader who will emphasize peace and yet, use his authority to conquer (control) nations. The Greek word for *conquer* in Revelation 6:2, means *to subdue*. This person will be a part of the seventh kingdom of prophecy that will continue for a brief time (Revelation 17:10, 11).

HOW PEACE CAN DESTROY

Destruction under the guise of peace was visible in Afghanistan. As long as the Afghans observed the strict laws of the Taliban, they were unharmed. If any person resisted or disagreed with even one small point of Taliban rule, they were met with swift "Islamic" justice. Crowds gathered in stadiums to watch people be shot, hung or have their hands amputated for such "evils" as having a television, owning a VCR, or stealing to feed their starving children, or a woman who exposed her face in public.

During his 42 month rule, the Beast and his kings will control all global economics and influence world political decisions. Those who differ or oppose their policies will be killed by beheading (Revelation 20:4). I am certain the Antichrist will take this verse from the Koran as his inspired reason for beheading the "infidels."

> I will cast terror into the hearts of the infidels. Strike off their heads, strike off the very tips of their fingers! That [is] because they defied God and his apostle (Surah VIII:12).

Those who submit to his plans, purposes and policies will be permitted to buy and sell, using a mark called the "mark of the beast" (Revelation 13:17). This mark on the right hand or forehead literally separates his followers from others who refuse the mark. Those rejecting the mark will be killed. The peace initiated by the Antichrist will bring survival to his followers and death to his enemies (Revelation 20:4).

According to Islamic tradition, the Mahdi will institute Islamic justice through peace. But his justice will be exacted by the sword of Islam. This means that anyone who rejects the Koran, or Mohammad as the prophet, and refuses to follow their strict, twisted concepts will be killed. Again, this accurately fits the description given by the Biblical prophets of the coming Beast and his kingdom!

THE ANTICHRIST—A HOMOSEXUAL?

Recently, I met a man from Jacksonville, Florida, who was born in Iran. His father had worked in the Persian

Gulf area for many years. This man had at one time served as a double agent for the U.S. government. He gave me some startling information that he had observed first hand while living in the Persian Gulf area.

Years ago, his father had been hired by a wealthy sheik to construct buildings in the country. I was stunned when he told me that about 80 percent of the men in this particular Islamic nation were bi-sexual or had been involved at some time in homosexual activity (men with boys). He said the women were completely covered from head to toe and only their eyes were visible. This bred a lack of natural affection toward women and caused young men to engage in sexual activity with young boys. Since there was no physical contact with women permitted, he believed this only added to the problem.

His story brought to mind two accounts related to me while traveling through the West Bank, in Israel. One of my Arab bus drivers, a Palestinian who had lived in the West Bank from his birth, informed me that in one major West Bank city, about 50 percent of the men were bi-sexuals and homosexuals. I was stunned! I asked him, "Are you certain?" He said "Of course." He then informed me that one of the highest ranking leaders of the PLO (Palestinian Liberation Organization) was a homosexual, and for years he had asked one of his friends to bring him young boys to have sexual relations with. Only in his later years did this PLO leader marry a woman in order to have a child to carry on his name.

This could be why the Bible identifies Jerusalem as the city which is "spiritually called Sodom and Egypt, where our Lord was crucified" (Revelation 11:8). Egypt loved slavery and Sodom was a city corrupted with sexual perversion, especially homosexuality (2 Peter 2:6-10). Apparently, bi-sexual and homosexual activity is common among some groups of Muslims, although it said to be forbidden.

This is not to say that most Muslims are homosexuals or that they approve of these acts; most Muslims would not. But those on the "inside," especially from Middle Eastern and Persian Gulf nations, reveal a strong weakness to bisexuality and homosexual activity.

The inspired prophet Daniel, again gives his readers an amazing insight into the Antichrist's feelings toward the opposite sex:

> Neither shall he regard the God of his fathers, nor the desire of women, nor regard any god: for he shall magnify himself above all (Daniel 11:37).

From this passage some have speculated that the Antichrist may be a homosexual. The term *no desire of women* infers his lack of interest in the opposite sex. While this verse does not explicitly state that this man will be openly gay, the fact is that if homosexuality is common in certain regions, it would not forbid this sexual orientation in the coming Antichrist.

Speaking of women, in many Middle Eastern and Gulf nations, women are not treated with the dignity and respect they would receive in the West. In most Islamic nations, women are forced to wear the traditional Arab and Islamic clothes (covering all but the eyes), and are often dominated and manipulated by their husbands.

Years ago I met with a gentleman who had worked with a large American oil company in one of the small Gulf States. Tony recalled an incident where a wealthy oil sheik had five wives. One wife had accidentally walked in front of him in public. After returning home, he demanded his other four wives watch while the woman was tied to a stake and burned alive. I thought to myself, "How can a man claim to love a woman and treat her in such a violent manner?" The answer is, there is no true love. The woman is nothing more than an object to gratify sexual pleasure and produce children.

The cruel treatment of women was seen during the Gulf War, when Iraq invaded Kuwait. The Iraqi soldiers raped every woman they could find. Some were raped multiple times and were then murdered. These women were not Jews or Christians, but Muslims!

Moderate and secular Muslims are often repulsed by how the fanatical Muslims mistreat their companions, or murder in God's name. My friends in Israel who have a Muslim background often remind me, "These people are not true Muslims." Yet, the fundamental Islamic mentality is pushing out the moderate, more open minded Muslims.

RADICAL CHANGES FROM 50 YEARS AGO

Turn the pages of time back 50 years. In the past, no known homosexual would have been accepted to serve in any important public office. Today, homosexuality is not only acceptable behavior but is being encouraged as an alternative lifestyle.

Fifty years ago, only two nations were considered the superpowers with weapons of mass destruction—America and Russia. Today, third world dictators trade drugs for weapons on the black market and can purchase almost anything the mind can dream. Today, France, Israel, India, Pakistan, England and other largely populated nations have the nuclear bomb. Almost every major Islamic nation is working on a nuclear program with hopes of having their own nuclear capability. This is the greatest threat to the existence of Israel.

Fifty years ago, no one was talking "land for peace" among the Israelis and the Palestinians. Peace efforts began under President Jimmy Carter and continued under President Bill Clinton, falling apart toward the end of his administration. Yet, the Palestinian cry is, "If Israel wants peace, you must give us land."

The presence of Christians and Jews in Jerusalem is a thorn in the side of fanatical Islam. The Islamic nations surrounding Israel are using the Palestinian issue to eventually push the Jews and Christians out of Jerusalem. For many years, Jews and Palestinians raised their families together and were friends. After Israel annexed East Jerusalem from Jordan after the 1967 War, attitudes changed. Later, the intifada (uprising) began, inspiring a plague of Islamic suicide martyrs.

The controversy of a Palestinian state separate from Israel will be the fuse on the bomb, igniting the entire area into an apocalyptic powder keg. I believe the man who many will claim as Islam's messiah, will be the man to fulfill many of the ancient prophecies regarding the Beast and his kingdom.

WHEN ISLAM RULES

After reading what we have written thus far, perhaps you understand why I believe the eighth and final kingdom that will seek Israel's annihilation will be a fanatical Islamic confederacy. What would it be like living under strict Islamic rule? What changes would occur?

The first changes an Islamic "messiah" would initiate are the laws governing religion and worship. These changes are alluded to in Daniel 7:25:

> And he shall speak great words against the most High, and shall wear out the saints of the most High, and think to change times and laws: and they shall be given into his hand until a time and times and the dividing of time.

Muslims call God *Allah* and not *Yahveh*, the Hebrew name of the God of Abraham, Isaac and Jacob. The future dictator will speak great words against the God of the Hebrews and Christians (Daniel 7:25, Revelation 13:6). As pointed out by many scholars, the name Allah is the form of a famous moon deity that was worshiped in pre-Islamic times.

Muslims consider Allah the same God of Abraham, Isaac and Ishmael, but the Arabic name *Allah* was not a name revealed to Mohammed but was already in existence in pre-Islamic times.

The Antichrist will change *times*. The word times can allude to changing the *year*, or the calendar. Islam uses a different calendar then modern western nations. We use a solar calendar that centers on Christ's birth. The Islamic calendar began in the year 622.

The second interesting point is that the West, and most modern nations, use a solar calendar that consist of 365.25 days in a complete solar year. The Islamic calendar is a lunar calendar with 354 or 355 days making a complete year.

The third point involves the day of worship. Hindus worship on Thursday, Muslims on Friday, Jews on Saturday and traditional Christians on Sunday. Under Islamic rule only one day, Friday, would be chosen to worship Allah. Any global Islamic leader would set out to change the "times and laws," three ways:

1. By changing the calendar to an Islamic calendar.
2. By changing the year from 365.25 days to 354 or 355 days a year.
3. By changing the day of worship to Friday, the Islamic day of worship.

This power to change *times* and *laws* is for a "time (one year), times (two years), and dividing of times (one half a year)," which totals 42 months (see Daniel 7:25; 12:7, and Revelation 12:13). He changes *times* and *laws*. While this could allude to the laws of Moses in the Torah, the Aramaic word here is *dath*, and in the context could allude to changing the religious laws. This interpretation agrees with the religious agenda of a global Islamic leader. According to Muslim tradition, the time will come when the entire world will be Muslim, an no other religion will be practiced.

What would it be like living under the rule of a fanatical Islamic dictator? This question can be answered by observing the conditions of modern nations whose governments are controlled by fanatical Muslims.

1. The first demand would be forced conversion or death.

In such nations as the Sudan and parts of Nigeria, armed Muslim warriors enter villages demanding the entire village to meet together. Those who convert to Islam are spared. Those who do not are killed to create fear. Often, the men are killed while the wives and daughters are raped and the children taken to be raised as Muslims. In Indonesia, more than 8,000 Christians were forced to convert to Islam or face death (Source: *Voice of the Martyrs* magazine).

2. The second requirement would be to destroy churches and synagogues.

Indonesia is the largest Islamic nation in the world, with 170 million people. While the president is a moderate Muslim leader, the radical Muslims, or jihad warriors, have killed more then 10,000 Christians in two years. At least 600 church buildings have been set on fire, bombed or destroyed since 1995.

While many moderate Muslims have gotten along with Christians for years, the rise of the fanatics is a serious threat to the stability of many Asian nations, including Indonesia.

3. The third requirement would be to conscript and retrain the youth.

When Christian youth are taken as captives, they are forced to convert or become slaves. If they convert they are sent to Islamic schools where they are taught the Koran and Muslim doctrine. While the Bible, the principle foundational book of America's documents, is banned from the public schools, in Islamic countries the Koran is taught in the school systems from the moment a child can read.

Muslims know that in order to win the next generation, they have to begin with the youth.

4. The fourth requirement would be to spread the message to new areas.

This task is to take the new converts and have them travel into other nations, taking with them the Islamic message. This missionary effort is supported with millions of dollars from Islamic nations, especially Saudi Arabia. Saudis provided 50 million dollars to organizations to help "evangelize" America for Islam.

Any religion has the right to proclaim its message to people, then allow the people to choose what they wish to believe. This is the universal method in which the Christian message is presented. Ministers preach a gospel message and conclude with an altar invitation. True Christianity never forces anyone to convert. Among the fanatical Muslims, no opportunity is given to reject the Koran or teachings of their prophet because rejection is the path to death. An article in the *A-Riyad* newspaper in Saudi Arabia explains the feelings of the fanatics:

> Israel was created by the Christian Church, believing that if for a blissful millennium the Jews were to rule Jerusalem, they would then return to Christianity. With imperialism embracing these fantasies, it built upon a state, concealing its Western infiltration. . . . The Zionist wet nurse will yet, in anguish cut off her breast and burn her last Bible as she faces a new wandering in the wilderness.

Hatred toward Israel, the West, Jews and Christians is a common thread in the fanatical communities. Among moderate Islamic countries, such as Jordan, Christians experience limited freedoms. Secular Muslims are often repulsed at the twisted thinking of many of their fellow Muslims. Among the Shiite branch of Islam, however, many Muslims blame America for the rebirth of Israel; they despise our support of the Jewish state. In their minds, if they can't defeat Israel, they will defeat America from within for supporting Israel.

HE WILL THINK HE IS GOD

The future Beast will become so lifted up in pride and manipulated by evil spirits, until he will believe he is God!

> He will oppose and will exalt himself over everything that is called God or is worshiped, so that he sets himself up in God's temple, proclaiming himself to be God (2 Thessalonians 2:4, NIV).

After this dictator invades Jerusalem, killing two prophets of God at the Temple Mount (see Revelation 11:3-7), the Antichrist will then take up a position on the Temple Mount, the third most sacred site to Islam. Imagine the rejoicing in surrounding Islamic nations the moment Jerusalem has been liberated from the hands of the Israelis!

During this time a second individual will join the team of the Antichrist. He is the false prophet who will build an image, or icon, to the Antichrist (the Greek word for "image" in Revelation 13 is *icon*, vv. 14, 15). Men from around the world will bow to the image and give allegiance in the form of worship to the Antichrist.

Solidifying the religious deception will be a series of miracles that will transpire in Jerusalem, but seen by the eyes of the world. These miracles are called by the apostle Paul, "lying signs and wonders" (2 Thessalonians 2:9). These counterfeit miracles will be so convincing, that Christ warned even the elect could be deceived (Matthew 24:24).

There are certain sects in Islam that perform varying supernatural "miracles." Ellie, my friend who was born in Iran, informed me that when she was a young girl living in Iran there was a sect of Muslims who practiced what Christians would term a form of sorcery. They were similar to psychics, and spent their time telling people their future.

One group could actually work themselves into a spiritual frenzy, then pierce their flesh with swords or sharp pieces of metal, and never bleed.

The Scripture informs us that one of the main miracles performed by the false prophet will be the supernatural ability to cause an icon of the Antichrist to actually come to life.

> And he had power to give life unto the image of the beast, that the image (icon) of the beast should both speak, and cause that as many as would not worship the image of the beast should be killed (Revelation 13:15).

In various parts of the world it is common to hear of religious statues weeping, or bleeding. While some consider this an amazing sign from God, I personally believe that these things are miracles of deception, since God forbids in his Word the use of any image of man, woman or beast with which to worship Him (see Deuteronomy 4:15-19).

It is possible these weeping, bleeding images are a way of preparing the world to accept the moment when the image of the beast will speak and live. To those deceived souls living on earth at that time, it will be a great sign that "God has come down among them."

Those who do not worship this image will be killed (Revelation 13:15). This indicates that the struggles and conflicts during the time known as the Great Tribulation (Matthew 24:21), will be more religious than political in nature. The Antichrist will set himself up as God, and will be worshiped. The false prophet, identified as the "lamb with two horns" (Revelation 13:11), will merge two major world religions together; apostate Christianity and Islam, and make their new religious headquarters in Jerusalem.

With Jerusalem as the new "Mecca," there will be no need for traditional "Roman Christianity;" therefore Rome will be burned with fire in one hour (see Revelation chapters 17 and 18). Since Rome, Italy, is the headquarters of the Roman Catholic Church and Rome represent historic Christianity, the beast and his boys will have no remorse in destroying the last symbol of the Christian faith on earth. This is alluded to in Revelation 17:16:

> And the ten horns which thou sawest upon the beast . . . shall make her desolate and naked, and shall eat her flesh, and burn her with fire. For God hath put in their hearts to fulfill his will, and to agree, and give their kingdom unto the beast, until the words of God shall be fulfilled.

PERSECUTION UNLIKE ANY OTHER TIME

The Beast kingdom will instigate the greatest season of persecution against Jews and those who convert to Christianity that has ever been in world history. This will produce the greatest number of religious martyrs in history (Revelation 6:9-11). Numerous prophecies speak of this time:

> But tidings out of the east and out of the north shall trouble him: therefore he shall go forth with great fury to destroy, and utterly to make away many (Daniel 11:44).

The phrase *make away many* means "to utterly slay and destroy." According to the Hebrew dictionary, it can also mean "to seclude and ban for religious reasons." The rage of the Beast is visible in his treatment toward the Jews.

> And his power shall be mighty, but not by his own power: and he shall destroy wonderfully, and shall prosper, and practice, and shall destroy the mighty and the holy people (8:24).

Notice the prophecy says, "not by his own power," because the power and authority the Antichrist receives will be from the power of Satan:

> And the beast which I saw was like unto a leopard, and his feet were as the feet of a bear, and his mouth as the mouth of a lion: and the dragon (Satan) gave him his power, and his seat, and great authority (Revelation 13:2).

The phrase *holy people* alludes to the Jewish people living in Israel. During the final 42 months of the beast kingdom, Daniel informs us:

> And at that time shall Michael stand up, the great prince which standeth for the children of thy people: and there shall be a time of trouble, such as never was since there was a nation even to that same time (Daniel 12:1).

Jesus described this same upheaval of humanity in Matthew 24, as "great tribulation." The wars and destruction will be so great that without divine interruption the entire human race would be in danger of extinction:

> For then shall be great tribulation, such as was not since the beginning of the world to this time, no, nor ever shall be. And except those days should be shortened, there should no flesh be saved: but for the elect's sake those days shall be shortened (Matthew 24:21, 22).

The Apostle Paul also spoke of this time of trouble and predicted:

> For when they shall say, Peace and safety; then sudden destruction cometh upon them, as travail upon a woman with child; and they shall not escape (1 Thessalonians 5:3).

The seven-year peace treaty initiates a false sense of security, as the nations declare, "Finally, peace and security!" Suddenly, the armies of the Beast invade northern Africa, controlling the sea lanes. His soldiers of jihad sweep into the rich oil nations of the Persian Gulf, seizing the black gold of the Arabian deserts. Israel will have been forced to disarm and the Antichrist will use the Palestinian cause to create a massive uprising on the streets inside of Israel, thus retaking East Jerusalem. He will station his command center in Jerusalem as indicated in Daniel 11:45:

> And he shall plant the tabernacles of his palace between the seas in the glorious holy mountain; yet he shall come to his end, and none shall help him."

Scholars indicate the *glorious holy mount* is Jerusalem or Mount Moriah. The word *seas* alludes to the Dead Sea and the Mediterranean Sea (Jerusalem is positioned between these two seas). Scripture says, "Then shall be a time of trouble" (Daniel 12:1), or "great tribulation" (Matthew 24:21).

At this time the words of Daniel 11:39 will be fulfilled, "He shall divide the land for gain." The Palestinians will be given the land they are demanding. Then, the predictions from the Koran and the Haddith will be reality. The Muslims will be permitted to "kill the swine (Jews) and destroy the cross" (anything representing Christianity).

This one man will turn against the Jews with a vengeance. Anyone who receives Christ during this season will be added to the Antichrist's hit list. Thankfully, this time of trouble will only last for 42 months. It will be interrupted by the return of the Messiah, Jesus Christ.

The peace treaty will be signed with Israel for one prophetic week, which is seven years (Daniel 9:27) The Beast and his armies invade Jerusalem in the middle of the seven years, known as mid-tribulation (Revelation chapters 11 and 13). He reigns from Jerusalem during the final half of the seven years and will be defeated by Christ who returns at the end of the seven years (Revelation 19:11-18).

If the Beast lives in Jerusalem the last 42 months, where will his throne of rule be during the first 42 months? After all, he will be the leader of a nation with an army. Islamic expectation may shed light on this question.

According to Islamic tradition, the Mahdi may be in hiding in the desert, in Iraq. Therefore Iraq is an important nation in the eyes of all Islam. Each year the Shiites celebrate the death of Ali and his 70 followers who were murdered in Iraq over 1,300 years ago. The nation of Iran would love to possess and annex Iraq, while expanding the Shiite version of Islam toward Syria, Lebanon and Israel.

I believe there is evidence that Iraq will be the area of main activity during the first 42 months of the Tribulation. Therefore, the Beast of the Bible will be the Beast from the same territory of ancient Babylon!

Ten

Future Headquarters of the Beast, Iraq

And the great city was divided into three parts, and the cities of the nations fell: and great Babylon came in remembrance before God, to give unto her the cup of the wine of the fierceness of his wrath (Revelation 16:19).

Named by the west, the Butcher of Baghdad, Saddam Hussein took control of Iraq in July, 1979. A Baathist, Saddam's vision for Iraq was one of power and grandeur. Fully aware of the historic significance of his nation, Saddam set in motion plans to rebuild the ancient city of Babylon, erect the world's largest mosque with the Euphrates river running though it and eventually become the leader of a new Islamic crescent that would include Israel as its prize possession. A lengthy war with Iran canceled many of his plans, but not before Saddam began spending millions of dollars rebuilding ancient Babylon.

THE MYSTIQUE OF ANCIENT BABYLON

After Noah's flood, men began to rebuild cities in the plains and valleys. One of the first of the many cities was Babel, built by Nimrod, the grandson of Noah through his son, Ham (see Genesis 10:1-10). According to Josephus, Babel was built on the plains of Shinar as an act of rebellion against God for sending the flood and destroying the world. Nimrod began erecting a tall tower, intending it to be so high that any future flood waters would never reach the top.

Josephus indicates that God destroyed the tower by sending a strong wind (Josephus, *Antiquities of the Jews*, 1.5.2). The tower was called "Tower of Babel," which can translate as "confusion," alluding to the incident where God scattered the people by confusing their languages. The modern area of Iraq became known in early history as Mesopotamia.

The next reference to the plains of Shinar is during the time of Abraham when a war was raging between four kings from Canaan and five kings from Mesopotamia. The Caananite army was led by Amraphel, king of Shinar (Genesis 14:1). The four allies listed in Genesis 14 are:

♦ Kedorlamour, king of Elam—this is modern Persia or Iraq

♦ Tidal, king of the nations—this was a king over Gentile tribes

♦ Amraphel, king of Shinar—this was the area of Babel

♦ Arioch, King of Ellasar— a city near Ur in Mesopotamia

The five kings from Mesopotamia ruled from the area of modern Syria and Iraq. Abraham, the father of the Hebrews, went to war against these five kings and reclaimed the possessions they had seized during the battle. Following his war victory, Abraham went to Jerusalem where he met with Melchizedek, the first priest of God (Genesis 14).

Abraham was involved in this battle with kings from the same area where Israel's worst enemies still live. Since 1979, the countries of Syria and Iraq have led the opposition against the Jews, against the rebirth of Israel, against the re-unification of Jerusalem and against the return of the Jews to their historic land.

Just as the kings surrounding ancient Babylon initiated the first conflict with the father of the Hebrew nation, the future Islamic kings of a new Babylon will instigate the final mother of battles that will climax in the valley of Megiddo in central Israel (Revelation 16:16).

After Abraham, the next mention in the Bible of the Babylonian area is found in the prophetic Book of Daniel. By this time Babylon was not just a city built on the Euphrates River, but had grown into a mighty kingdom, overpowering Mesopotamia.

It extended its dominion by conquering Israel and Jerusalem. Many Jews were carried away captive to Babylon for 70 years, including Daniel the prophet. It was the Babylonian armies who destroyed Solomon's Temple, seizing the priceless vessels of gold and silver, storing them in the treasure houses of Babylonian gods (Jeremiah 52).

Ancient Babylon (the area of Iraq today) was eventually seized by the armies of the Medes and Persians in about 546 B.C. Many years later, the Grecian empire under Alexander the Great conquered the Persians and took possession of Babylon. They extended their global dominion into more countries.

Following the Grecians, the Roman Empire began to form and eventually became the fourth kingdom in Daniel's prophecies (Daniel 2:40; 7:23).

Hundreds of years later, in the seventh century A.D., the Arabs would possess the land of Shinar and set up the headquarters of various branches of Islam near the banks of the Euphrates river. In fact, in A.D. 637, the first Arab empire was established in Mesopotamia. The first Arab government was called the Abbasid Empire.

THE ARABIANS TAKE BABYLON

Throughout history the Babylonian area was occupied by the Sumerians, Assyrians, Chaldeans, Persians and Greeks, but never by the Arabians. A prophecy in Isaiah implies that the Arabians would be there; but after Babylon's destruction, they would no longer live there:

> And Babylon, the glory of kingdoms, the beauty of the Chaldees' excellency, shall be as when God overthrew Sodom and Gomorrah. It shall never be inhabited, neither shall it be dwelt in from generation to generation: neither shall the Arabian pitch tent there; neither shall the shepherds make their fold there (Isaiah 13:19, 20).

This prophecy of destruction must allude to the present, since the Arabians did not pitch their tents there until 637. Between A.D. 661 and A.D. 750, the Arabs conquered the town of al-Kufa, which was situated near the ruins of ancient Babylon. This town became the capitol of Iraq and the headquarters for the Umayyad dynasty.

Between 744-750 the Islamic caliph, Marwan II ibn Muhammad transferred his residence to Harran, Iraq. Beginning in 717, fanatical caliphs began to persecute the Jews living in and around Babylon. Throughout Islamic history, the fate of the Jews often depended upon who the regional Islamic governor was at the time.

In A.D. 850, the Islamic caliph al-Mutawakkil, a religious fanatic, demanded Jews to wear a yellow head covering. The poor and servants had a yellow patch attached to the clothes on their chests or backs. During the early centuries of Islam, Jews and Christians were often forced to wear yellow clothing with patches on them, identifying them. In most instances, Jews and Christians were levied with heavy taxes.

Clearly, the plains of Shinar, the tower of Babel, the city of Babylon and the Kingdom of the Babylonians have played a major role in Biblical history and prophecy.

Iraq and the city of Baghdad have served as headquarters for caliphs in Islam since the infancy of the religion. Just as the first battle of Abraham, the father of the Jews, involved the king of Mesopotamia (Iraq), the final battle of battles involving Israel and her enemies will be with a future King of Iraq. Prophetically, he will be the king of the neo-Babylon.

The New Babylon-Rising From the Ashes

On October 11, 1990, the *New York Times, International Edition* said:

> Under Saddam Hussein, one of the ancient world's most legendary cities has begun to rise again. More than an archaeological venture, the new Babylon is self-consciously dedicated to the idea that Nebuchadnezzar has a successor in Mr. Hussein, whose military prowess and vision will restore to Iraqis the glory their ancestors knew when all of what is now Iraq, Syria, Lebanon, Jordan, Kuwait and Israel was under Babylonian control.

The ancient king Nebuchadnezzar left instruction for the future of Babylon on cuneiform script tablets. On these clay tablets the scribes, 2,500 years ago, instructed those who find the tablets to rebuild the temples and palaces. This message was so clear to Saddam that during the ensuing major building project he had bricks impressed with his image and that of old king Nebuchadnezzar!

One Iraqi archeologist, Shafqa Mohammad Jaafar, said, "Because Babylon was built in ancient times and was a great city, it must be a great city again in the time of our great leader, Saddam Hussein." According to Paul Lewis of the *New York Times*, the motivation for rebuilding Babylon was to strengthen Iraqi nationalism by appealing to history. It also portrayed Saddam in the eyes of his people as the new Nebuchadnezzar, a leader who eventually conquered the world in his day.

After spending 100 million dollars, thousands of workers laid 60 million bricks along new walls in the new Babylon. Every six feet along the wall there is a brick with an inscription in Arabic saying, "The Babylon of Nebuchadnezzar was reconstructed in the era of Saddam Hussein." After laying 60 million bricks, rebuilding gates, walls and palaces, the last Babylonian festival was held in 1988. The war with Iran had taken its toll on Iraq and the building program ceased. Instead, Saddam began placing hundreds of millions of dollars into his lavish palaces, scattered throughout the country.

Saddam's invasion into Kuwait was not for oil or its oil deposits. Iraq has huge amounts of the world's reserves. The "spiritual" motive was to begin annexing the land that once belonged to ancient Babylon. It would have also given Iraq a much needed coastline.

Even the name "Babylon" is constantly in the minds of Iraqis. In the early 90's, Saddam built a super gun with a 16-inch barrel that was 172 feet long. The gun was tested, and set a new world record by shooting a projectile 112 miles straight up. The super-gun was code-named *Baby Babylon* by the Iraqis.

A second gun was being built when the parts were intercepted by special agents. The gun had a 39 inch barrel and was 512 feet long with a potential range of hundreds of miles. This larger gun was being named *Big Babylon!*

THE DEMISE OF SADDAM

Saddam Hussein, the Butcher of Bagdad, is finished. Like Hitler and the evil dictators before him, Saddam's rule will come to an end. He will never become the leader of the new Islamic crescent or the new king of Babylon. Yet, in the future, with Saddam removed and the country under different leadership, the ancient land of Shinar (Iraq) could once again expand with wealth from the oil wells and be rebuilt into a strong nation.

After all, the Bible teaches of a season of false peace. This peace must involve Israel and her Arab/Muslim neighbors. Yet, out of this region of the world will arise the leader of the new Islamic republic, a Muslim who will be received by the Islamic world at first, but in the end will be the most violent, blood-thirsty human to have ever walked. According to Paul this mans appearance is now being restrained, but one day he will be revealed in his full identity (2 Thessalonians 2:1-10).

IRAQ WILL BE THE HEADQUARTERS OF THE BEAST

Modern Iraq was once the center of the ancient Babylonian Empire. Bagdad served as the headquarters and center of operation for several Islamic dynasties. Today, the Shiite branch of Islam needs a headquarters; and I believe that Iraq, in the future, could become the center for Shiite Muslims who will claim this prophetic territory.

Since the Antichrist does not invade Israel until the middle of the seven-year period, he will be living and ruling from another nation prior to making his move against Israel. The prophet Daniel was told, "He (the Antichrist) will become great with a small people" (Daniel 11:23). His authority is identified through the symbol of a *little horn* (Daniel 7:8). These predictions reveal that for the first 42 months, the Antichrist will not be a well-known, powerful leader. For example, he will not necessarily be an elected official over the EU in his beginnings, but will control a small number of people. He will gain his power through deception and demonic control.

An indicator that Iraq will be heavily involved in this end-time, prophetic conflict is found in Revelation. John tells of activity involving the Euphrates River and a massive, 200-million-man army that will cross the river and pass through Iraq.

The Euphrates Connection

The Euphrates and Tigris rivers divide Iran from Iraq. The Euphrates begins in Turkey not far from Mount Ararat. It travels through Turkey, Syria and Iraq. and empties into the Persian Gulf (1,700 miles long).

The Euphrates was the eastern boundary of the Roman Empire. This river is the only river mentioned by name in prophecies related to the final days of the rule of the Beast kingdom. Biblically, several powerful, ancient spirits that have been bound in this great river, Euphrates, will be released during the Great Tribulation:

> Saying to the sixth angel which had the trumpet, Loose the four angels which are bound in the great river Euphrates. And the four angels were loosed, which were prepared for an hour, and a day, and a month, and a year, for to slay the third part of men (Revelation 9:14, 15).

These wicked angels will rise up and motivate a massive army of 200 million soldiers that will slay a third of mankind during a 13-month period. I personally believe these angels are the same ancient prince spirits that once ruled from the past empires of prophecy. These include the spirit of Babylon, the spirit of the Medes and Persians (mentioned in Daniel 10:13), along with the prince spirit of Greece (v. 20).

The above-mentioned empires all ruled from ancient Babylon; and according to Daniel, each kingdom had strong demonic spirits dominating it (Daniel 10). Later, toward the conclusion of the Tribulation, the Euphrates River will dry up to make a way for a massive army, headed by the kings of the East:

> And the sixth angel poured out his vial upon the great river Euphrates; and the water thereof was dried up, that the way of the kings of the east might be prepared (Revelation 16:12).

In Revelation, John indicates severe drought and famine will precede this event (6:8; 11:6). Presently, during the dry season the water level of the Euphrates may drop as low as 24 inches. The country of Turkey has constructed several massive dams which can presently shut off the flow of the Euphrates like a knob on a faucet.

Why is the emphasis on the Euphrates so important? Because ancient Babylon was built along the Euphrates, and Baghdad, the capitol of Iraq, sits near the Tigris River, not far from the Euphrates. If the Euphrates dries up and a massive army marches across, they will march from the area of Iran, Afghanistan and Pakistan, nations which are located east of the Euphrates.

These three nations are home to millions of Islamic radicals, all promoting their fanatical agenda.The Antichrist will be "great toward the east" (Daniel 8:9), which includes these Islamic-controlled areas mentioned above. Armies marching from the east would need to pass through Iraq, as they proceed into Israel and the valley of Megiddo.

We cannot underestimate the historical, spiritual and political importance of the Iraqi nation. No country on earth has more potential for massive biological and chemical weapons capabilities. No other land mass, other than Israel, has a richer prophetic history. To summarize Iraq:

- It is where the Tower of Babel was built.
- It is the site of the first global religion and first world government (Genesis 11).
- It was the cradle of civilization, and the area where Abraham lived (a place called Ur) before migrating to the Promised Land (Genesis 11:31).
- It was home to the five kings with whom Abraham and his servants fought (Genesis 14:1-8).
- It is the area where three major empires of Bible prophecy set up their kingdoms and have ruled.
- It occupies the territory of ancient Babylon.
- It is located in the center of the 10/40 window.

172/ Unleashing the Beast

- It was once the headquarters for the Shiite Muslims.
- It is where Al-Hussien, Mohammad's grandson, was murdered.
- It is the land of the Euphrates River.
- It is located east of Israel, where the Antichrist will be strong.
- Iraq, Syria, Kuwait and Lebanon united will form the old Babylon.
- It is the area where many Muslims believe the 12th Imam disappeared.
- It is where Muslims say the Mahdi will re-merge to take possession of the world, forming an Islamic empire.

It is not necessary for a future Iraqi ruler to continue rebuilding the ancient ruins of Babylon. The *spirit of Babylon* will be released during the Tribulation, and will work in the heart of the Beast and his 10 kings. This new Babylon will eventually consist of the areas encompassed by Iraq, Syria and Lebanon.

The Main Argument Against Neo-Babylon

Scholars may argue that ancient Babylon has been destroyed, and the Bible says it will not be rebuilt. According to Mike Coleman, this is one of the reasons Saddam desired to rebuild Babylon—to prove the Bible wrong! Throughout the Old Testament, the prophets gave grave warning about the utter destruction of Babylon. Many references are found in Jeremiah 50 and 51:

> Therefore the wild beasts of the desert with the wild beasts of the islands shall dwell there, and the owls shall dwell therein: and it shall be no more inhabited for ever; neither shall it be dwelt in from generation to generation(50:39).

> And thou shalt say, Thus shall Babylon sink, and shall not rise from the evil that I will bring upon her: and they shall be weary. Thus far are the words of Jeremiah (Jeremiah 51:64).

In Jeremiah's time Babylon invaded Israel, destroyed Jerusalem, burned the Temple and led the Jews captive. Jeremiah predicted the utter destruction of Babylon; yet, his prophecy parallels the prophecy in Revelation 17 and 18 concerning "Mystery Babylon." Jeremiah's Babylon is a political nation and John's Babylon is a religious system.

Prior to the Gulf War, I was on a plane with a rabbi from Hungary. We discussed the coming Gulf War. He believed Jeremiah alluded to that war with Iraq. The rabbi noted:

1. Jeremiah said a nation from the north would rise against Babylon (Jeremiah 50:41). The Medes and Persians that over-threw Babylon were from the east; America is called "North America."

2. Jeremiah said many kings would be raised up from the coast of the earth (Jeremiah 50:41). The largest coalition in history was raised up in the Gulf War.

The rabbi then showed me in Scripture where the Babylon of Jeremiah 51 was a future Babylon, or the area of modern Iraq. He noted that the original Babylon was never destroyed in the manner we read about in Jeremiah's prophecy. Ancient Babylon slowly deteriorated into ruins and rubble. Jeremiah said that the Babylon he saw would be destroyed by a "destroying wind" (Jeremiah 51:2). He noted that "bright arrows" would be used (Jeremiah 51:11), and the "reeds would be burned with fire" (Jeremiah 51:32). The Rabbi said:

> During the Gulf War, America or Israel may be forced to use nuclear weapons (the destroying wind), or arrows tipped with powerful weapons that will burn the area with fire (missles). If this prophecy does not happen in this war, it will in the future, and old Babylon will be destroyed.

If the headquarters of the Antichrist will be Iraq and the area of ancient Babylon, then at what point in time would this area be destroyed? It could be devastated during a war with Israel or the West, and rebuilt for the Antichrist.

After all, the nations of the earth would never allow Iraq to be destroyed without demanding the West to rebuild it completely, just as we did Japan and Germany after World War II.

Since John, in Revelation, sees "Mystery Babylon" burn up with fire in one hour, and this prophecy is fulfilled during the final 42 months of the Great Tribulation, Iraq could become the command center for the Beast kingdom during the first 42 months. Following a major conflict with the king of the north—Turkey (see Daniel 1:40-44)—the area of Iraq could be destroyed and the Antichrist would then make his move into Israel.

Without doubt, Iraq will become the center of attention in the last days. Just as Jerusalem is the gate of heaven and the place where God placed His name, ancient Babel was the gate of wickedness and the place where deceit and spiritual corruption was birthed (see Zechariah 5:5-11).

The battles in the future, especially against Islamic terrorists, will eventually change the face of nations on the earth. Iraq will be one of those nations. Iraq's prosperity is based on oil; and oil will play a huge role in the final kingdom.

Eleven

WHO CONTROLS THE GOLD AND THE OIL?

He shall enter peaceably even upon the fattest places of
the province; and he shall do that which his fathers have
not done, nor his fathers' fathers; he shall scatter among
them the prey, and spoil, and riches: yea, and he shall fore-
cast his devices against the strong holds, even for a time
Daniel 11:24.

On February 8, 1999, the Dow Jones launched an Islamic Market index to track companies whose businesses
operate in line with Islamic principles. It tracks 600 stocks
from 300 companies with total market capitalization of
$7.5 trillion.

The Book of Revelation clearly reveals that future wars,
plagues, famines and global confusion will not only ad-
versely impact humanity, but such circumstances will also
create chaos in the financial markets. A major earthquake

in a nation's economic center will send fault lines of panic rippling through the marketplace. This may be why the prophet Daniel indicated the Antichrist would focus on seeking after gold.

> But in his estate shall he honor the God of forces: and a god whom his fathers knew not shall he honor with gold, and silver, and with precious stones, and pleasant things. But he shall have power over the treasures of gold and of silver, and over all the precious things of Egypt: and the Libyans and the Ethiopians shall be at his steps (Daniel 11:38, 43).

Note that he will have power over the gold and silver. He will also honor the God of forces (war) with gold, silver and precious stones. Recently, a report was released revealing how many rich Muslims were beginning to invest their money in gold, silver and gem stones. The fear is that a national collapse of a major economy would make the paper money worthless. Another purpose for this exchange may be based on Islamic tradition.

Some Muslims believe that the only currency that will survive the last days will be coins minted of gold and silver. The interest in such currency is being headed up from the region of Malaysia and Indonesia. The objective is to mint gold and silver coins, called the Dinar (gold) and Dirham (silver), and eventually make them the official currency of a new Islamic empire. These coins are already being produced in 22 Islamic nations, and they are free from government fiat and financial interest. The Islamic party of Klantan, a party of 500,000 people in Northeast Malaysia, began heading up the project a few years ago.

The currency is based on Mohammad's saying that was remembered by Abu Bakr, the man who compiled Mohammed's teachings into the Koran after the prophet's death: "A time is certainly coming over mankind in which there will be nothing left which will be of use save a dinar and a dirham" (The *Musnad* of Imam Ahmad ibn Hanbal).

In the late 1990s, the concept of the gold and silver Islamic coins was discussed with the mufti (Islamic spiritual leader) in Egypt. He approved of the concept and said:

> All Islamic transactions should be done in gold and silver. This will lead to a powerful establishment of an Islamic economy capable of facing up to the international economic blocs.

Other Islamic leaders have hailed the idea of a unified Islamic currency based upon gold and silver:

> The Islamic Dinar is a newly created 100 percent gold currency that its backers hope and believe will become the currency of more than one billion Muslims. The organizers of this currency not only see the Islamic Dinar as an eventual rival to the U.S. Dollar as a reserve currency, and are hopeful it will usher in the demise of the U.S. Dollar.

> This will be the money in the pockets of the people. It will not replace currency but will not be used for usury! Charging interest to fellow Muslims is supposed to be forbidden (*Source*: http://www.gold-eagle.com/editorials_98/taylor112598.html).

Islam's motivations are rooted in its history. Dr. Mahathir bin Hohamad said to fellow Muslims in a speech he made in Kuala Lumpur on June 25, 2001:

> Muslims must never forget that we missed the Industrial Age completely. We have practically no industrial capacity because when the Industrial Revolution was taking place we could not decide whether it was compatible with Islam or not. In the end we were left behind and found ourselves totally dependent on the industrialised countries for our needs, including of course our defense needs.

> Today we see the rapid advance of the Information Age. Whether we like it or not it is going to have a tremendous impact on our society and on our religion. We cannot isolate or insulate ourselves from the Information Revolution and the technology which is driving it. Our economy will certainly be affected by it.

CONTROLLING THE GOLD

History has proven that when adverse economic trouble (such as the Great Depression) strikes a nation, gold and silver bars and coins become the economic nest egg to investors. During the Carter presidency when the interest rates skyrocketed, the price of gold and silver soared. With any major event that rattles the global economic markets, gold and silver begin to rise.

For example, from July 2001 to May 2002, the price of gold rose from $270 an ounce to almost $320 an ounce, an increase of nearly $50 an ounce. Several years ago, the Bank of England chose to sell a large amount of their gold bullion. Interestingly, it was purchased by a Muslim who chose to buy all of the hoard! After the sale, the bank chose to keep the remaining portion for the time being.

When the Twin Towers of the World Trade Center collapsed, it was revealed that huge amounts of gold were in the basement. There was a concern by the owners that the tremendous heat may have melted some of the gold. Later, the gold was discovered and transferred by heavy security to an unspecified location. The owners of this gold were Saudi Arabia and Kuwait, both Islamic nations.

Under President Clinton, the price of gold and silver began to fall with the sharp rise in the stock market. Investors felt more money could be made in less time in the stock market. As the new millennium approached and fears of Y2K computer failures swept the globe, concerns caused some to move a small amount of their portfolio to gold and silver coins. The no-show of Y2K made investors feel secure, but eventually the Internet bubble burst and stocks began to decline. The bull went south.

America's currency was once backed by the gold standard. For every hard currency printed, there was sufficient gold to back it up. America came off the gold standard, and today our currency is backed by the strength of the Federal Reserve and the confidence of the American people. If America experiences more terrorist attacks of the magnitude of September 11, 2001, it is possible we could experience an economic setback of major proportions.

The Antichrist will control the treasures of gold and silver, and will honor his god with gold, silver and precious stones. It is clear that the Islamic world is already moving into the direction of eventually forming the strongest economic currency in the world by owning the gold and silver.

The nations in the Persian Gulf region are more than able to purchase countless amounts of gold, silver, and precious stones. Their wealth has come from the "gold buried in the sand." Often called the "treasure chest of Allah," the rich, dark oil hidden in the sands of the Arabian Desert has padded the coffers and filled the bank vaults of the descendants of Ishmael and Esau as nothing else.

I have said for many years that any man who could own and control the oil wells of the Arabian Peninsula could control the entire world. Prior to the Gulf War when Saddam invaded Kuwait, his desire was to annex the small country back into Iraq. Since he had his own millions pouring in from oil wells, he was not interested in owning Saudi Arabia and bringing the wrath of the Arab world on his head.

In fact, I was told by a reliable source that the United States had trained a special unit that was already in Iraq and ready to "take out" Saddam. When the King of Saudi Arabia was told this plan, he protested and said it would cause repercussions and destroy Arab pride. As a result, the secret mission was called off, the unit never made it out alive, and this war ended. Had Saddam moved into Saudi Arabia before the allies had the time to form the coalition, then he could have controlled the faucet on the oil wells. He could have named his prices and retaliated against

America by limiting or cutting off the supply. In the future, the Antichrist will place the world in checkmate by controlling the oil wells in the desert. This is revealed through a word study in the Book of Daniel:

> He shall enter peaceably even upon the fattest places of the province; and he shall do that which his fathers have not done, nor his fathers' fathers; he shall scatter among them the prey, and spoil, and riches: yea, and he shall forecast his devices against the strong holds, even for a time (Daniel 11:24).

Notice this man will enter peaceably. Those dwelling in the country will accept him without a struggle. The phrase "fattest places of the province" is a strong clue that I believe alludes to controlling the oil states. The word "fattest" comes from the Hebrew root word *shemon*, which is the word for oily, or oil.

Today, we would say that he is over the places of oil, or the oil wells. Saudi Arabia is the leading Middle Eastern nation producing oil in today's world. The word "province" is the Hebrew word *medina*. The interesting aspect of this word is that a famous city in Saudi Arabia is called Medina. The city of Medina is the second holiest city to the Muslims and is where the founder of Islam, Mohammed, is buried.

During the Gulf War, there was a controversy over foreign troops fighting on the soil of Saudi Arabia. The extremist Muslims believed the soldiers from the West were infidels who were polluting the purity of the land of Mohammed. This anger boiled in private, motivating such organizations as bin Laden and the al-Qaeda terrorist network.

Bin Laden was expelled from Saudi Arabia because his personal opinions were creating contention and because of possible danger to the royal family. The fanatical segments of Islam found in Iran, Iraq and Syria would rejoice to see the royal family and the oil wells cut from the hands of the moderate Arabs and given over to the power of fanatics who would then hold the West hostage.

THE PRESIDENT WAS RIGHT

When President Bush suggested America should be less dependent on Middle East oil and begin exploration in Alaska or some other area, the environmentalists arose to block his goal. A major news network had the senator from Alaska on their program; but prior to the interview, they showed pictures of the pristine land where the administration proposed that drilling be done. The senator immediately rebuked the network for showing pictures not from Alaska!

The facts are that the area being considered was about the size of Dulles Airport in northern Virginia, and the oil had already been located. I have never understood why a senator in the northeast should have any say so about what the people in Alaska want! Americans, by and large, don't like change and don't like to upset the status quo.

Our national slogan should be "If it's ain't broke, don't fix it; and if it is broke, don't tell me about it." Americans do not enjoy solving a problem before it happens, a hypothetical situation. But we love pointing the finger of blame at everyone else after the problem comes. It seems few politicians are interested in losing votes among the environmentalists; but they enjoy floating along.

Yet, if America does not become more independent from Middle Eastern oil, we will find a man in the future who will cut off the oil to the West, thereby birthing a disaster. By owning much of the gold and silver and the gold in the sand of the Persian Gulf states, the nations of the world must come to him for their supply.

The Scripture indicates that this man, the Antichrist, will set up a system of buying and selling, thus controlling even the common people.

The Mysterious Mark of the Beast

The apostle John alludes to an unusual economic plan the kingdom of the beast will initiate. Christians call this system of buying and selling the "Mark of the Beast."

> And he causeth all, both small and great, rich and poor, free and bond, to receive a mark in their right hand, or in their foreheads: and that no man might buy or sell, save he that had the mark, or the name of the beast, or the number of his name (Revelation 13:16, 17).

Throughout the centuries, Christian scholars have researched and debated the issue of what this mark actually is. People receive authority to purchase and sell goods if they have one of three things: the mark of the beast, the name of the beast and the number of his name

The entire world is marked by numbers. Americans have a Social Security number, a telephone number, a street number, zip code and various credit card numbers. We are known more by our numbers than by our names. In fact, most information cannot be released publicly unless a person has a pin number or a secret pass number.

Revelation 13:18 says the number of the beast can be calculated to 666. Since numbers are already used for buying and selling, it is not difficult to see how the number of the beast would work through a computer system.

The name of the beast is more difficult to understand, yet people who worship this man as though he were a god will use his name to obtain special favors. The mark of the beast, issued by the false prophet, will be placed on the right hand or the forehead.

The mark is actually a religious mark that publicly identifies a follower of the Antichrist and his religion. Just as Hindus have a red dot in the center of their forehead, the false prophet of Revelation 13:11-16 will cause men and women to receive the mark.

Whatever system is developed, the global grip of the Antichrist, for 42 months, will be so strong that nations who do not submit to his control will be forced into starvation or face the consequences of war. At that time in history, the plagues, famines, droughts and strange cosmic disturbances will have disrupted the planet and limited the food supplies, fresh water supplies and clean air (Revelation 6:4-8).

Gold and oil will be the two economic keys that will unlock the power of the Antichrist. Up to this point, no one has been able to combine them both for a weapon of power. One man, followed by 10 other kings or national leaders, will one day understand the power of the gold and the oil. When he rises, the world will know it!

Twelve

THE MANIFESTO
OF THE ANTICHRIST

When the Antichrist sets up his kingdom and assumes his power, he will not be a man without a plan. An unbelieving world will look on with awe at his prowess. The Antichrist will have a seven-point agenda that I call the Seven-Phase Manifesto of the Antichrist. I will outline this agenda and make a few brief comments on each item.

PHASE 1: TAKE CONTROL OF ISRAEL

THE PROPHECY

> And he shall plant the tabernacles of his palace between the seas in the glorious holy mountain; yet he shall come to his end, and none shall help him (Daniel 11:45).

To defeat the Jewish state and seize possession of the ancient high places (the West Bank), Judea and Samaria is a necessity for the Palestinians.

Phase 2: Take Control of Jerusalem

The Prophecy:

> They shall fall by the edge of the sword, and they shall be
> led away captive into all nations: and Jerusalem shall be
> trodden down of the Gentiles, until the times of the Gen-
> tiles be fulfilled (Luke 21:24).

Since the destruction of the Jewish Temple and Jerusalem in 70 A.D., Jerusalem has changed hands among Gentile empires. From the Romans to the Byzantines, to the
Muslims, to the Crusaders, to the Turks, to the British,
and finally, to the Jews, Jerusalem has been occupied for
over 1,900 years.

But prophecy indicates the Gentiles will take possession of Jerusalem one more time. The Scriptures outline
Satan's plans and schemes, as he tries one last time to
wrest control of the earth from God and from Jesus Christ.

Phase 3: Convert the World
to His Own Religion

The Prophecy:

> And they worshiped the dragon which gave power unto
> the beast: and they worshiped the beast, saying, Who is
> like unto the beast? who is able to make war with him?
> (Revelation 13:4).

For centuries, Europe and the Middle East were hotbeds
for forced conversions. When the Roman Church leaders ruled,
Spanish Jews were forced to convert or face expulsion and,
in some instances, death. When radical Islamic forces ruled,
Jews faced terrorism and Christians faced martyrdom.

Forced conversion will become common during the Tribulation, and those who refuse will face the final solution: death.

PHASE 4: DESTROY ALL OPPOSITION
TO HIS CONTROL

THE PROPHECY

> But tidings out of the east and out of the north shall trouble him: therefore he shall go forth with great fury to destroy and to utterly make away many (Daniel 11:44).

> And I saw thrones, and they sat upon them, and judgement was given unto them: and I saw the souls of them that were beheaded for the witness of Jesus, and for the word of God (Revelation 20:4).

The Antichrist will show no mercy to those who oppose his rule and his religion. The avenue of punishment will be to behead those who resist him. In anger and wrath he will take lives.

In the beginning, he made a peace treaty with many (Daniel 9:27), and at the end of his rule, he will go forth to destroy many. The blood of Christian martyrs will become the seed that will bring the wrath of God upon the earth, and, eventually, destruction to the Beast kingdom.

PHASE 5: CONTROL ALL BUYING
AND SELLING

THE PROPHECY

> And he causeth all both small and great, rich and poor, free and bond, to receive a mark in their right hand, or in their foreheads: and that no man might buy or sell, save he that had the mark, or the name of the beast, or the number of his name (Revelation 13:16, 17).

Prophecy indicates an extensive famine during the final seven years prior to Christ's return (Revelation 6:5-6). This famine will impact entire nations and continents, thus creating the need for food rationing. Forty-two months into the tribulation, a controlled system of buying and selling will be introduced by a religious leader, identified as the false prophet (Revelation 16:13; 19:20). A mysterious religious mark will be placed on the right hand or on the forehead of those following the Antichrist and the false prophet. Those rejecting this new system of economic control will be subject to martyrdom.

PHASE 6: CONTROL THE TEMPLE MOUNT IN JERUSALEM

THE PROPHECY

> And there was given me a reed like unto a rod: and the angel stood, saying Rise, and measure the temple of God, and the altar, and them that worship therein. But the court which is without the temple leave out, and measure it not; for it is given unto the Gentiles: and the holy city shall they tread under foot forty and two months (Revelation 11:1, 2).

The Temple John was told to measure was not a Temple in heaven, but a future Temple that will be erected in Jerusalem during the first 42 months or the first part of the Tribulation. The only place the Jews would construct a Temple would be on the site of the previous two Temples, the Temple Mountain in Jerusalem.

Islam will not permit a Jewish house of worship without a war. The Antichrist will be restrained in his rule and unbridled authority during the first half of the Tribulation, giving the two witnesses time to minister to a Jewish remnant.

After God's supernatural restraining power is removed, this "man of sin and son of perdition" will be unleashed upon the nations. His main assignment will be to free the Temple Mount from the hands of the infidel Jews. After his invasion, the holy city (Jerusalem) will be trodden down by the Antichrist armies for 42 months.

PHASE 7: BE WORSHIPED AS GOD

THE PROPHECY

> Who opposeth and exalteth himself above all that is called God, or that is worshiped; so that he as God sitteth in the temple of God, showing himself that he is God (2 Thessalonians 2:4).

> And they worshiped the dragon which gave power unto the beast: and they worshiped the beast, saying, Who is like unto the beast? Who is able to make war with him? (Revelation 13:4).

Why would so many people desire to worship a man? Today, there are imams, Hindu holy men and gurus that are literally worshiped as though they are gods. One such Islamic man is from France and 20 million of his Shiite followers claim he is the incarnation of God.

The fact that the Antichrist will be a military warrior and none will be able to make war with him will cause his followers to treat him as a god.

Thirteen

COSMIC SIGNS AND
LAST DAYS PROPHECY

They shall fall by the edge of the sword, and shall be led away captive into all nations: and Jerusalem shall be trodden down of the Gentiles, until the times of the Gentiles be fulfilled. And there shall be signs in the sun, and in the moon, and in the stars; and upon the earth distress of nations, with perplexity; the sea and the waves roaring: men's hearts failing them for fear, and for looking after those things which are coming on the earth: for the powers of heaven shall be shaken. And then shall they see the Son of man coming in a cloud with power and great glory. And when these things begin to come to pass, then look up, and lift up your heads; for your redemption draweth nigh (Luke 21:24-28).

Saddam Hussein sat silently in his private palace, surrounded by the most noted astrologers Morocco had. The Iraqi dictator had brought in these men from another country to assist him in a special astrology reading. Did the position of the stars tell a secret? Would Saddam be defeated in the coming Gulf War, or would he be victorious? According to inside sources, the Arab stargazers determined that the stars of heaven were on Saddam's side. Like the false prophets in 2 Chronicles 18 who gave King Ahab ill-fated prophecies of victory, Saddam was told he would defeat America and eventually defeat Israel.

The stars were wrong and so were those interpreting them. I am certain that a few heads rolled after Saddam's Iraqi armies were crushed by the coalition. The Bible speaks of the utter nonsense of believing the stars in heaven can influence and govern your private life:

> Thou art wearied in the multitude of thy counsels. Let now the astrologers, the stargazers, the monthly prognostica-tors, stand up, and save thee from these things that shall come upon thee.

> Behold they shall be a stubble; the fire shall burn them; they shall not deliver themselves from the power of the flame: there shall not be a coal to warm at, nor fire to sit before it (Isaiah 47:13, 14).

This type of venture, known as astrology, is a belief that the position of the stars at certain times induces the effect of good or bad luck in your daily routine. While astrology and star worship is forbidden in Scripture, there is a study of Biblical astronomy that can reveal clues to Biblical signs in the heavens as they pertain to the last days. These are the signs in the sun, moon and stars that Christ spoke of in Luke 21:25-28.

For Signs and Seasons

> And God said, Let there be lights in the firmament of heaven to divide the day from the night; and let them be for signs, and for seasons, and for days and for years (Genesis 1:14).

The sun, moon and stars were created for more than to simply give light to mankind. Prior to calendars, the sun determined the cycle of the day and year; and the moon determined the cycle of the month. Most primitive cultures used a solar calendar, but Jewish seasons were determined by a lunar calendar. In the circuit of the heavens, there are 48 star bodies recognized as constellations.

Jewish rabbinical sources point out that for 2,500 years, men had no written record of the words of God. According to historians such as Josephus, God gave to the first man, Adam, the secrets of the universe. Adam then passed these heavenly mysteries on to his son Seth—whose sons passed them on to their children, including one of the first prophets in the Bible, Enoch.

Josephus also wrote that God revealed to Adam the earth would be destroyed twice: once by a volume of water, and again by a judgment of fire.

> They also were the inventors of that peculiar sort of wisdom which is concerned with the heavenly bodies and their order. And that their inventions might not be lost before they were sufficiently known, upon Adam's prediction that the world was to be destroyed at one time by the force of fire and another time by the violence and quantity of water, they made two pillars; the one of brick, and the other of stone: they inscribed their discoveries on them both, that in case the pillar of brick should be destroyed by the flood, the pillar of stone might remain, and exhibit those discoveries to mankind; and also inform them that there was another pillar of brick erected by them. Now this remains in the land of Siriad to this day. (Josephus; Antiquities of the Jews, II.3).

Adam's prediction of a global flood occurred in Noah's time, around 1,658 years after the creation of Adam. Adam's second warning, forecasting the destruction of the earth by fire, is also predicted in 2 Peter 3:7. This is called by theologians "the renovation of the earth with fire."

If we are to understand the true purpose of the heavenly signs, we must not embrace the perversion of personal astrology. Instead, we must discover the original intent of God's creation, and see how God stamped a unique, visible picture of the progression of His story in the heavens. Our comprehension should include the ability to perceive times and seasons by recognizing how God's people understood these things before pagan corruption perverted their understanding.

Numerous times in Scripture, the sun, moon and stars became a visible picture of a future prophetic promise:

+ Abraham was told his seed would be as the "stars of heaven" (Genesis 22:17).

+ Joshua was given the heavenly sign of the sun staying in one spot (Joshua 10:13).

+ Hezekiah was given the sign of the sundial going backwards (Isaiah 38:8).

+ The Magi saw a star in the east as the sign the Messiah was born (Matthew 2:2).

TWELVE MAJOR CONSTELLATIONS

I believe Adam, Seth and Enoch recognized that the constellations in the heavens held a mysterious redemptive story, placed there as a visible reminder of God's plan. It appears that 4,000 years ago, ancient nations (China, Chaldea, Egypt) all used the same names and meanings of the stars in the heavens.

Eventually, through idol worship, the Babylonian and Greek myths brought corruption in both the names and meanings. These star pictures, created originally by God, are symbolisms that represent things to come.

For example, out of 48 constellations, there are 12 major ones that the sun passes through during a solar year.

Jacob, the father of modern Israel, had 12 sons who were the titular heads of the 12 tribes of Israel. These tribes eventually formed the nation of Israel (see Genesis 35:22).

In chapter 37, Jacob's youngest son, Joseph, experienced a prophetic dream in which he saw the sun, moon and stars of the heavens bowing before him (Genesis 37:9). Jacob interpreted his son's dream to mean that he (Jacob), Joseph's mother and the 11 other brothers would bow before Joseph (Genesis 37:10).

The 11 stars were symbols of the 11 constellations in heaven, with Joseph representing the 12th. Some Jewish scholars believe that the 12 tribes were given an emblem connecting each tribe with one of the 12 major constellations.

An example related to the tribes is the symbol for the tribe of Judah. Genesis 49:9 reveals that Judah's tribal emblem is a lion. In the heavens, one of the 12 major constellations is a lion known as Leo. The sun begins its yearly circuit in constellation of the virgin (Virgo) and the year ends in the constellation Leo, the lion.

These two heavenly symbols, a virgin and a lion, reveal the beginning and the conclusion of Christ's ministry. He was born of a virgin (Isaiah 7:14), and He will become the Lion of the tribe of Judah (Revelation 5:5). Notice a prophecy given by Jacob to his son Judah:

> Judah is a lion's whelp: from the prey, my son, thou art gone up: he stooped down, he couched as a lion, and as an old lion; who shall rouse him up? The sceptre shall not depart from Judah, nor a lawgiver from between his feet, until Shiloh come; and unto him shall the gathering of the people be (Genesis 49:9-10).

In his book, *Jesus Christ Our Promised Seed,* author Victor Wierwille writes:

> Jacob by inspiration declares that Judah is symbolized by the lion. In the 12 constellations of the (heaven), there is

one sign for the lion and that is Leo. Here in Genesis 49, Leo the lion and Judah are being identified with each other. Further, Jacob declares that "the scepter shall not depart from Judah, nor the lawgiver from between his feet."

In astronomical terms, this statement is also significant because of the star named Regulus, which is the dominant, brightest star in the constellation of Leo. The Arabic word *regel* means foot and is identical to the Aramaic word *rega* and the Hebrew word *regel*. Thus the brightest star in the constellation of Leo has the Biblical connotation of the foot, tying in with "from between his feet" of Genesis 49:10.

In this one verse alone, the Lion of Judah, Leo, is intertwined with a lawgiver coming from between his feet, represented by the king star Regulus."

Note that all ancient civilizations recognized Regulus as the king star. The word *regulus* means "kingly" in the Latin. Therefore, this single star was considered the only king star in the heavenly constellations.

Another example showing the connection of Biblical symbols to the signs in the heavens is Revelation 1:16. John saw Christ in heaven holding seven stars in His right hand. These seven stars represent the pastors of the seven churches listed in Revelation 2 and 3 (see Revelation 1:20). There were certainly more than seven leading churches at the time John wrote this.

Why did Christ choose these particular seven churches to receive His prophetic message?

History reveals that the seven churches mentioned in Revelation 2 and 3 were all located in Asia Minor, or what is today modern Turkey. All were located at the base of the Taurus Mountains. The parallel is this: In the heavens, there is a constellation called Taurus, the bull; in the ancient Jewish Temple, a bull offering was designated for the high priest (Leviticus 3:6-14).

Within the constellation Taurus is a star cluster called the Pleiades. It consists of a main star surrounded by seven other stars. The word Pleiades means "congregation of the ruler." The Arabic name is al-Cyclone, meaning *center*, because ancient Jews and Arabs considered the Pleiades the center of the universe.

How significant it is that the Pleiades, with one star surrounded by seven others, is in the constellation Taurus, and the seven churches were located at the base of the Taurus Mountains! (The Pleiades is mentioned in the Bible in Job 9:9 and Job 38:31). Christ had seven stars in His right hand, and He addressed the seven churches. We can see that this vision of Christ has a parallel star picture in the heavens.

The prophetic symbolism found in the Book of Revelation can correspond to certain heavenly constellations. The woman with child (Revelation 12:1, 2) is a picture of Virgo the virgin. The great dragon (Revelation 12:3) could allude to Draco, the dragon. The ram (lamb) with two horns (Revelation 12:11-16) and identified with the false prophet could be parallel to the star formation called Aries, the ram. Christ is called the Lion of Judah (Revelation 5:5); the constellation called Leo is identified as a lion. It appears that some of the veiled symbols John saw in his revelation were heavenly symbols the people of his day were familiar with.

Types of Cosmic Signs

With this concept in mind, let us attempt to interpret the various prophetic signs in the sun, moon and stars. Seven types of cosmic signs are mentioned in prophecies throughout the Bible:

- A sackcloth sun (Revelation 6:12)
- A bloody moon (Revelation 6:12)
- Great signs in the heavens (Luke 21:25)

- ◆ Fearful signs in the heavens (Luke 21:11)
- ◆ Stars falling from the heavens (Matthew 24:29)
- ◆ A darkening of the constellations (Isaiah 13:10)
- ◆ The powers of heaven are shaken (Luke 21:26)

Luke quoted Christ as warning of great and fearful signs in the heavens (Luke 21:11). These signs would involve the sun, moon and stars. Let us begin with the sun and explore thoughts related to strange cosmic activity in the sun.

THE SIGNS IN THE SUN

Christ indicated there would be signs in the sun. According to Biblical prophecy, during the seven-year Tribulation, we are told the sun will be darkened:

> And the sun became black as sackcloth of hair, and the moon became blood (Revelation 6:12).

> Immediately after the tribulation . . . shall the sun be darkened. (Matthew 24:29).

> The sun and the moon shall be darkened, and the stars shall withdraw their shining (Joel 3:15).

When I read this as a child, I imagined the sun going completely black, or supernaturally burning itself out. In the early 1990s, a war in the Persian Gulf gave me another perspective on this prophecy. During the Gulf War, black smoke from hundreds of oil well fires poured into the blue skies over Kuwait, causing the sun to appear to be veiled in blackness.

Observers in the surrounding areas also noted that the chemicals released in the atmosphere by the fires created an illusion that caused the moon to appear to be blood red. The prophet Joel, more than 2,500 years ago, predicted:

> The sun shall be turned into darkness, and the moon into blood, before the great and the terrible day of the Lord come (Joel 2:31).

Could the billowing smoke, veiling the sun, and the red moon be an allusion to what Joel saw in a vision thousands of years ago? Or is there another application to the sun being darkened and the moon turning into blood? After the Gulf War, I learned that many rabbis believed that a sackcloth sun, or the sun being darkened, could suggest a complete solar eclipse.

The rabbis taught that a solar eclipse is a bad omen for the world. Rabbi Meir made another observation when he said, "When the luminaries are in eclipse, it is a bad omen for Israel." According to the rabbinical interpretations of eclipses, a solar eclipse is a sign of trouble for the world and a lunar eclipse is a sign of trouble for Israel. No more than seven eclipses can occur in one year.

Twice in the 20th century there were seven total eclipses. Both years, 1917 and 1973, were filled with prophetic implications. During the seven eclipses that occurred in 1917:

- The Russian Revolution occurred, introducing communism, and World War I was coming to an end.
- Occurring in December, the seventh eclipse coincided with General Allenby liberating Jerusalem from 400 years of Turkish rule.
- The Belfour Declaration was signed, giving the Jews access back to Palestine.

During the seven eclipses that occurred in 1973:

- The Yom Kippur War occurred, which could have destroyed Israel.
- The Arab oil embargo impacted America and the West.
- Twenty-eight nations suffered from drought.
- History's largest explosion occurred on the surface of the sun.

Since Israel is on a lunar calendar—based on the cycles of the moon—any eclipse on the moon is considered a cosmic sign for Israel. The moon has a $29^{1/2}$-day cycle. In slightly less than 30 days, the moon enters a four-phase cycle as it moves from darkness to light, and back to darkness. According to Avi Ben Mordechai, in his book *Signs in the Heaven*, with each cycle of nearly 30 days the ancient rabbis understood that the moon was being reborn, or "born again."

In the Old Testament period, an entire Jewish festival was proclaimed at the beginning of the month, called the *B'rit Chadasha*, or the New Moon Festival. During the 1,000-year reign of Christ, the New Moon Festival will be reinstituted (Isaiah 66:23).

THE MOON OF BLOOD

The inspired Bible prophets predicted that the moon would become blood (see Acts 2:20). For centuries, scholars have attempted to ascertain the meaning of this prophecy. After America's moon landing in the late 1960's, some suggested this verse could refer to a war on the surface of the moon between America and Russia.

Again, an understanding of Jewish beliefs may help explain the possible meaning of this unusual prediction. In 1996, Israel celebrated the 3,000[th]-year anniversary of Jerusalem—from King David's conquest in 1004 B.C. to A.D. 1996.

On Passover, April 3, 1996, a full lunar eclipse appeared over Jerusalem. A photograph of this eclipse appeared in the *Jerusalem Post* with the caption, "The Moon of Blood." This phrase caught my attention. When a full lunar eclipse appears, the moon takes on a reddish, almost bloody appearance.

On September 26 of the same year, a second lunar eclipse created a blood-like image and was visible in Jerusalem on the eve of the Feast of Tabernacles. A third lunar eclipse (90%) happened six months later during Purim, the celebration to remember how the famed Jewish Queen Esther defeated the wicked plans of Haman.

Thus, three lunar eclipses occurring within one year on or near three Jewish celebration days is almost unheard of. These three "blood moons" caused excitement among the rabbis in Israel. The fact that a blood moon appeared twice the same year and fell on the first and last feast of Israel indicated to them that this was a cosmic sign from God of impending trouble in Israel. The ancient belief was that a blood moon (lunar eclipse) could symbolize bloodshed and war. Since 1996, thousands of Israelis have died in their own land from the suicide attacks of Islamic radicals.

From a Hebraic understanding, the signs of a sackcloth sun and a blood moon can refer to a full solar and lunar eclipse. According to the Scriptures, this will be one form of cosmic activity prior to the coming Day of the Lord and the future Tribulation (Acts 2:20).

ECLIPSE OVER EGYPT

When the final Islamic dictator forms the eighth kingdom, he will invade Egypt. We read about this in Daniel 11:43 and in the book of Ezekiel. The Bible reveals unusual cosmic activity during this time.

> And when I shall put thee out, I will cover the heaven, and make the stars thereof dark: I will cover the sun with a cloud and the moon shall not give her light (Ezekiel 32:7).

> The bright lights of heaven will I make dark over thee, and will set darkness upon the land saith the Lord God (Ezekiel 32:8).

This prophecy has two possible interpretations. First, these clouds may form through massive explosions of weapons and bombs, whose aftermath fills the skies with dark suffocating pillars of smoke and gas. This would create a dark cloud covering over both the sun and the moon.

The second possibility is that the prophecy could refer to darkness caused by a complete solar eclipse. A scripture found in Ezekiel predicts a time when the king of

Babylon (a type of antichrist) will come, as Nebuchadnezzar did centuries ago, and conquer Egypt. Ezekiel 30:4-6 says that Ethiopia and Libya will fall into the conflict. These three nations, Egypt, Libya and Ethiopia, will be conquered and controlled by the future Antichrist (see Daniel 11:43). The Ezekiel prophecy reads:

> At Tehaphnehes also the day shall be darkened, when I shall break there the yokes of Egypt: and the pomp of her strength shall cease in her: as for her, a cloud shall cover her, and her daughters shall go into captivity (Ezekiel 30:18).

If the fulfillment of this prophecy is linked to a solar eclipse, there are two eclipses that will cover this area mentioned with darkness. The first one is on October 3, 2005 at 12:50 p.m. Cairo time, and another on March 29, 2006 at 11:52 a.m. Cairo time. Dr. J. H. Hertz makes an interesting observation related to the March 29, 2006 eclipse. According to him, the ninth plague to hit Egypt in the time of Moses happened on the first of Nisan.

March 29, 2006 is the first of Nisan on the Jewish calendar. On this date and at this particular time, there will be a 114-mile path of total darkness in the very area mentioned by Ezekiel. Of course, there will be other future eclipses, but these are the more recently predicted. Such research by Christian astronomers helps them examine the evidence to see if there is a connection to Biblical prophecy, and the possible time of its fulfillment.

SIGNS OF THE PLANETS

One of the strangest petitions in Scripture is when King Hezekiah requested that the shadow of the sundial go backwards ten degrees (2 Kings 20:11). In order for this to happen, it would necessitate a shifting in the rotation of the earth, and that would cause a global upheaval. Ancient historians Berosus and Seneca said this is what occurred.

Plato ascribed the conflagrations of the world to the action of a "celestial body that, changing its path, passed close by the earth." This may be why in about 701 B.C., the ancient global calendars changed from a 360-day-a-year calendar to a calendar with five extra days added each year. For an additional five days to be added, some drastic change had to occur.

At the time of the Exodus 3,500 years ago, a series of ten plagues struck Egypt. An ancient papyrus, written on both sides, was found in Memphis, Egypt, near the pyramids. In 1828, it was acquired by the museum of Leiden in the Netherlands, and Alan Gardnier translated it in 1909. The papyrus was a lamentation that revealed the horror and ruins of Egypt. The information in the scroll dealt with Upper Egypt, the same area where the Hebrews lived and eventually made their exodus.

In his book, *Ages in Chaos,* author Immanuel Velikovsky believes the papyrus alludes to the plagues that struck Egypt at the time of the Exodus. The plagues of Egypt included three days of darkness (Exodus 10:21), large hail stones (Exodus 9:24) and rivers turning into blood (Exodus 7:20). In Upper Egypt, the fields and cattle were devastated (see Exodus 9:25, 10:15). These plagues were God's judgment being unleashed against the unbelieving, idolatrous Egyptians who held the Hebrews in captivity.

Numerous secular historians wrote of strange and horrible plagues that struck the earth about the same time that the exodus was under way in Egypt. Some scholars point out that a massive comet passed by the earth about the time that God opened the Red Sea. In *Natural History,* Pliny wrote that it was "a terrible comet . . . (that) was twisted like a coil, and it was very grim to behold." The *Jewish Talmud* reports that stones fell in Egypt and were very hot. An Arabian writer from the ninth century named Masudi related the tradition of this catastrophe and told of swift clouds, ants and other signs of the Lord's rage when many perished in Mecca.

In *Ages of Chaos,* author Immanuel Velikovsky writes about "plagues of insects, drought, and earthquake in the night . . . clouds sweeping the ground, (and) a tidal flood carrying away entire tribes. These disturbances were experienced in Arabia and Egypt alike."

Whatever method God used to judge the Egyptians, the impact was felt as far away as Arabia. Astronomers seem to think the Egyptian catastrophe was rooted in some form of a heavenly activity, perhaps by a comet passing close to the earth's orbit. In early history, the planets were considered wandering stars. Modern science acknowledges the existence of nine planets, but the early Hebrews recognized only seven planets. The seven-branched candlestick in the ancient Jewish Temple was a picture of the seven planets. Called the menorah, it consisted of seven gold branches filled with olive oil that provided light for the holy place:

> The Temple . . . had in it three things that were very wonderful and famous among all mankind: the candlestick, the table (of shewbread), and the altar of incense. Now the seven lamps signified the seven planets; for so many there were springing out of the candlestick (*Josephus, War of the Jews,* V.5).

Alignment at the Time of Creation

Modern computer software can now trace the position of the sun, moon and stars in history as far back as 3996 B.C. According to some models, the seven planets were in a straight line at the time of the creation of Adam. This alignment was similar to the seven lamps sitting on top of the menorah.

According to computer models, a similar alignment occurred the year that Sodom and Gomorrah was destroyed, and on August 3, 70 A.D. when the Temple was destroyed.

On December 1, 1997, the moon and eight of the planets lined up in a straight line. This alignment lasted for eight days and occurred during the Jewish celebration called Hanukkah, also known as the Feast of Lights. From west to east it was Pluto, Mercury, Mars, Neptune, Jupiter and Saturn.

A similar alignment occurred again in May 2000. This string alignment is a noted event in secular history. For example, the Chinese calendar began about 1953 B.C., with a planetary alignment in which all of the visible planets were lined up next to the sun. This same alignment was repeated on May 5, 2002. On this day in Bethlehem, at the Church of the Nativity where Christ was born, a siege was underway involving local Islamic militants.

During May, 2002, another cosmic sign appeared in the sky over Bethlehem. On April 1, 2 B.C., the planets Saturn, Venus, and Mars formed a triangular conjunction that could be seen in Israel. On May 5, 2002, another triangular conjunction occurred with three planets, and was visible in Israel. It appeared to be directly over the Church of the Nativity in Bethlehem.

It is possible that the cosmic signs that introduced the birth of King Messiah may be repeating themselves to introduce the return of the King!

The planetary alignments were once thought to create dangerous stress on the earth, but scientists have discovered that the pull of the planets is too far away to have any impact on earth. Therefore, they serve only as a sign, or a visible indicator of prophetic parallels.

Fourteen

MORE SIGNS
IN THE HEAVENS

In early history, the planet Mars was recognized by the Romans and Greeks as a planet of war. Among the Hebrews, the planet Jupiter had a special meaning. The Hebrew name is *Tzedeq*, which means "righteous one." It was called the Star of David and it represented kingship, coronations and the birth of kings.

In 1994, a cosmic event involving Jupiter excited both astronomers and rabbis. A comet known as the Shoemaker-Levi comet broke into 21 pieces. For seven straight days, from July 16 to July 22, a series of 16 fragments from the comet began to bombard the surface of Jupiter. These impacts caused explosions much larger and more powerful than the nuclear bombs dropped on Japan during World War II. They covered an area that was much larger than the diameter of the Earth.

Hebrew researchers indicate that, according to Jewish tradition, when the planet Jupiter is hit in the heavens, it is a sign of the end of the world. It is also strange that the beginning of this cosmic activity was the 9th of Av on the Hebrew calendar. This was the anniversary of the destruction of both Jewish Temples in 587 B.C. and A.D. 70. Note also that the bombardment occurred on the same day that secret talks to discuss exchanging Israel's land for peace were being conducted in Oslo, Norway.

Since the planet Jupiter was considered to be the planet representing King David, and he was given the promise of a throne in Jerusalem, the bombardment of Jupiter can be interpreted as a sign of future strikes on Israel, Jerusalem and the Jewish people. Certainly the end-time Biblical prophecies speak of a time of "Jacob's trouble" (Jeremiah 30:7).

This phase alludes to the 7-year Tribulation period when Israel will experience one more assault from the offspring of Ishmael as they aspire to reverse the blessing of the birthright God imparted to Abraham's seed through Isaac and Jacob. This historic family feud between the Hebrews and their Arab cousins will climax during this final seven years of Tribulation that is recorded in Daniel 9:27.

The Appearance of Comets

Throughout secular history, comets have been considered a bad omen. They often appear several years before a major war or natural disaster. In ancient history, nations would not enter into battle after a comet was observed.

One of the first comets to ever be named was discovered by Sir Edmund Halley. Named Halley's comet, it reappears approximately every 78 years. Researchers note that this comet appeared in 12 B.C. at the time Herod was extending the Temple platform in Jerusalem. It reappeared in A.D. 66, four years prior to the destruction of Jerusalem and the Temple.

In the twentieth century, the comet streaked through the heavens in 1910, just four years prior to the outbreak of World War I. More recently, the comet was visible on earth in 1986, just four years before the conflict in the Persian Gulf. I believe these time frames are more than just a mere coincidence. It appears that God is giving a visible heavenly warning of what is coming each time this comet streaks through our galaxy, entering earth's view.

The appearance of comets has been interpreted as an omen of future trouble. For example, on August 9, 1974, the comet Kohoutek was in our solar system. During that time, all nine leaders of the Common Market fell, and President Nixon departed from office. On the Hebrew calendar, August 9 was the 9th of Av, the most dreaded and negative day of the year among the Hebrew people.

Let me point out that neither the planets nor the stars are creating these negative effects on earth; this idea would be utter nonsense. But, this unique activity in the heavens appears to be a visible indicator, revealing prophetic seasons on earth.

THE HALE-BOPP COMET

The initial discovery of this large comet was on April 27, 1993. On the Hebrew calendar this was the 6th of Iyar. Forty-five years prior, on the same day, the British Mandate over Palestine ended. On our calendar this date was May 15, 1948, the official day Israel was re-birthed as a nation.

On August 2, 1995, the pre-discovery images were found on plates taken at the Anglo-Australian Observatory that showed the comet was active. It was spotted again on July 23, 1995 in the constellation Sagittarius, the half-man, half-beast constellation (perhaps a picture of the coming Antichrist). It was reported that the comet was 50 times brighter than Halley's comet.

The Hale-Bopp comet was eventually seen by the human eye during the entire year of 1998. According to Christian astronomers such as Bob Wadsworth, the last time this comet was seen was when it passed by the earth about 4,200 years ago. This would be about the time Noah began building the ark. Bill Cloud, founder of Shoreshim Ministries, states that according to the *Seder Olam Rabbah*, an ancient Jewish text, a comet appeared in the heavens at the time that Noah was building the ark.

Imagine, some 4,200 years later, seeing the same comet that was visible at the time when Noah was warned the flood was coming! Jesus said in Matthew 24:37-39, "But as the days of Noah were, so shall the coming of the Son of Man be." The cosmic sign of Noah's day was again repeated in our generation.

On May 20, 1997, the Hale-Bopp comet entered Orion and had exited it by June 16. The comet was positioned in Orion during the Jewish Feast of Pentecost (June 11, 1997). In 1998, it was reported in Israel that, according to Jewish oral tradition, when a comet was seen passing through Orion, it was a sign that the earth would be destroyed. The combination of the bombardment of Jupiter and the huge Hale-Bopp comet created a stir among prophetic students who endeavor to discern the signs of the times (Matthew 16:3) and the signs in the heavens (Luke 21:25).

An additional note, when the Hale-Bopp comet was visible on earth, it was the year 5758 on the Jewish calendar. Each letter of the Hebrew alphabet has a number value, and the numbers can be interchanged as letters of the alphabet. The name Noah in Hebrew is two letters, *Nun* and *Het*. The numerical value of Nun is 50, and the value of Het is eight. Therefore, the Hebrew name Noah totals 58. How unique that the comet Noah witnessed in his day reappeared unexpectedly 4,200 years later at a time when the last two numbers on the Jewish calendar spell Noah in Hebrew!

THE MEANING OF FALLING STARS

It may seem strange to many that Hebrew astronomic investigators have noted that major prophetic events are also connected to falling stars or meteorite showers. When any strange cosmic activity happens on a Jewish feast day or other noted season marking Jewish history, it is taken as either a good or bad omen, depending upon how the ancient teachers viewed the previous patterns of such activity in history.

One day during the Jewish year that is considered the worst day in Hebrew history is the 9th of Av. According to Jewish tradition, the following bad events occurred on the 9th of Av:

- The 10 spies brought an evil report to Moses.
- The first Temple (Solomon's) was destroyed by the Babylonians.
- The second Temple, built by Zerubbabel, was destroyed by the Romans.
- In A.D. 71, the Romans plowed the city under with salt and destroyed the third Temple (Herod's).
- The messianic hero, Shimon Bar Kochba, and his men were destroyed.
- England expelled its entire Jewish population in A.D. 1492.
- Twenty-one huge meteorites hit Jupiter in 1994.
- A huge meteorite shower hit Earth in 1997.

In his historical writings, the Jewish historian Josephus gave a list of the strange and supernatural signs that occurred four years prior to the destruction of Jerusalem:

The signs were so evident and did plainly foretell their future desolation...Thus there was a star resembling a sword, which stood over the city, and a comet that continued a whole year...on the feast of unleavened bread on the eighth day of Nisan at the ninth hour of the night, so great a light shown round about the altar and the holy house, that it appeared to be bright day time; which lasted for an hour...At the same time a heifer, as she was led to sacrifice, brought forth a lamb in the midst of the temple.

Moreover, the eastern gate of the inner court of the temple, which was of brass, and vastly heavy, and rested upon a basis armed with iron, and had bolts fastened very deep into the first floor, which was made of entire stone, was seen to be opened of its own accord about the sixth hour of the night. Those who kept the Temple came running to the captain of the Temple, and told him of it: who then came up hither, and not without great difficulty, was able to shut the gate again (Josephus, *Antiquities, War of the Jews*).

These series of cosmic signs began occurring four years prior to the actual destruction of Jerusalem and the Holy Temple. The comet that passed through in the year A.D. 66 was believed to be Halley's comet. The most unusual cosmic sign was the "star that was shaped like a sword." Naturally this was interpreted as a sign of war with the Romans, and the eventual defeat of the Jewish revolt. The meaning of the "star shaped like a sword" has been a mystery until recently.

During a meteorite shower in Italy in 1998, a photograph of it displayed the falling stars fashioning the shape of a large sword in the heavens! (Center section). Four years prior to Israel's war with the Romans that led to Jerusalem's demise, the star like a sword was a cosmic warning of impending danger. Four years prior to America's war on terrorism, and approximately four years prior to the Catholic Church experiencing its worst internal conflict in hundreds of years, a meteorite shower formed a sword over Italy!

In November of 2001, another meteorite shower, the Leonid shower, occurred. This time the cosmic dust appeared to be falling from the paw of Leo the lion. As stated earlier, the lion is the emblem of the tribe of Judah. Christ is identified as the "lion of the tribe of Judah" (Revelation 5:5).

This meteorite shower also formed the shape of a long sword in the sky. Was the sign that Josephus recorded, the star shaped like a sword, a meteorite shower that was visible over Jerusalem? If so, we are experiencing a repeat of the same type of signs.

One may say, "Hasn't there always been comets, eclipses and meteorite showers? What is so important about these?" These are important because they are falling on Hebrew feast days and are happening during times when other Biblical prophecies are being fulfilled. Some, such as Hale-Bopp, have a pattern associated with the days of Noah. Since Jesus said there would be signs in the sun, moon, and stars, then we must be aware of these signs and understand how to properly discern them.

At the time of the birth of Christ, there were wise men from Persia and Babylon called Magi. These men were trained to scrutinize the alignment and position of the planets in the constellations. When certain planets were positioned within certain constellations, it was understood as a sign of a coming war, or possibly the birth of a king. Such was the case when the Magi came to King Herod and announced the birth of a Jewish king. These astronomers had seen His star in the east (Matthew 2:2).

The star they saw was likely a conjunction of certain planets that created a very bright star in the heavens. Astronomers note that on August 12, 3 B.C., Jupiter (the king star) and Venus (the morning star) were in conjunction. Any conjunction with Jupiter was considered a sign of the birth of a leader or royalty. Due to the corruption of astronomy that was birthed by astrology, the true understanding of the signs in the heavens was lost and the myth-seekers and star-gazers took the symbols of the twelve constellations and began applying them to the personal, daily lives of people.

After hundreds of years, Christian researchers are now reexamining and revisiting the original meaning of the stars and their signs. Such a book is W. E. Bullinger's *Witness in the Stars*. The stars in the sky are a visible word picture of the progression of God's revelation of Jesus Christ.

Many of the symbols used in the Book of Revelation—the lamb with two horns, the dragon, the virgin woman in travail, and the lion—are all part of the ancient symbols connected to major constellations. (This is discussed in more detail on my video series, *Unlocking Revelation*.)

THE SIGN OF THE GRAND CROSS

Prior to the new millennium, a total solar eclipse over the Middle East was interpreted by some as a sign of the time of the end. On August 11, 1999, a total solar eclipse occurred over Israel. In Europe and the Middle East, from start to finish, it lasted from 12:00 p.m. to 3:00 p.m., about three hours. At the time of the eclipse, four planets—Mars, Saturn, Jupiter, and Uranus—were positioned in such a manner that, if a person were to draw an invisible line from one planet to another, it would form an X-shaped cross.

Called a "Grand Cross," this unique sign becomes more interesting when you consider the time in which the eclipse and the positioning of these four planets occurred. Christian astronomers point out that on Passover, April 28 in A.D. 28, the same four planets were in a similar position to form a Grand Cross. Some scholars believe this was the time of the crucifixion.

If April 28 in A.D. 28 is the first day, and we move forward using the ancient 360 day a year prophetic calendar, then 2,000 years later (720,000 days) the date is August 11, 1999, the same day the three-hour eclipse occurred from 12:00 p.m. to 3:00 p.m. The New Testament notes that as Christ hung on the cross, there was darkness upon the earth for three hours, from the third to the ninth hour (Luke 23:44). This was from 12:00 p.m. to 3:00 p.m. Both days fell on a Wednesday.

One of my secular Muslim friends in Jerusalem told me that Muslims living in Jerusalem and the West Bank fell into great fear when this eclipse occurred. Many remained locked in their homes, praying. Some who were very illiterate believed this was a sign the world was coming to an end and the day of judgement was about to arrive. Other Muslims believe a tradition that a time of great darkness will precede the day of judgement.

How interesting it is that the sign of the Grand Cross, a unique positioning of four planets, was seen in darkness as the sun was hidden for three hours, stretching from the Middle East into Europe! The next day, August 12, 1999, the new moon was visible at sunset. This first day of Elul on the Hebrew calendar begins a period of 40 days of repentance that concludes on Yom Kipper, the Day of Atonement.

Perhaps the eclipse was a reminder of the darkness the earth would enter, and the Grand Cross was a reminder that our faith in the Cross of Christ is our only solution. The answer for humanity is to repent of sins and accept the redemptive work of Christ. A month later, Israel celebrated its New Year on September 11.

TARGET DATE: SEPTEMBER 11

The plan was set and the strike date was September 11. Immediately following the breaking news reports from New York, my office was inundated with a myriad of e-mails and phone calls, asking if we had inside information about what was happening and why. The question kept coming up, "Why was September 11 selected?"

Is this date special in the Islamic religion? Was it linked to American history? Many Islamic terrorist attacks have occurred in the month of September:

- September 6, 1970—Palestinian militants hijacked four different airliners in one day.

- September 5, 1972—Black September terrorists executed an attack at the Olympics
- September 10, 1976—Croatian terrorists hijacked a TWA airliner.
- September 23, 1983—An Omni Gulf airbus was brought down by a bomb.
- September 20, 1984—Islamic radicals bombed the U.S. Embassy in Beirut
- September 11, 2001—Terrorists flew airplanes into the Twin Towers and the Pentagon

The month of September has been marked as a month for terrorist attacks. Often, the Jewish New Year, Rosh Hashanah, falls in the month of September.

THE STAR THAT LED THE MAGI

While nobody is certain about the actual birthday of Christ, scholars note that the Magi came to see Him in Bethlehem after "seeing His star in the east" (Matthew 2:2). These Magi were possibly chief men of the Persian religion. They were among six tribes of the Medes. In history, they would have interpreted the dreams of the Persian leaders and were noted for their genuine knowledge in the natural and spiritual realms. They were also familiar with the astronomical phenomena.

There was also a religious belief among the Persians that three deliverers would come. Two would be prophets who would reform the world and raise up a kingdom, and a third would rule the kingdom and raise the dead. These men may have been influenced by the Jewish Scriptures and history left in their nation after the Jews returned from Babylonian captivity. The Magi's reference to "his star" may be this verse:

> I shall see him, but not now: I shall behold him, but not nigh: there shall come a Star out of Jacob, and a Sceptre

shall rise out of Israel, and shall smite the corners of Moab, and destroy all the children of Sheth (Numbers 24:17).

Because the Hebrew prophet Daniel held a high position in the Persian Empire, I am certain the wise men of the Medes and Persians were familiar with Daniel's prophecies concerning the future of Israel. These prophecies, along with the predictions in the Torah, gave these men an understanding that a king Messiah would one day be born in Israel. Daniel was set in command over the wise men in his time (Daniel 6:3).

So, it was a cosmic occurrence in the heavens that precipitated the interest of the Magi in journeying to Israel to visit the infant child destined to be the King of the Jews. It appears this mysterious star was actually formed by some type of planetary conjunction that developed within one of the major constellations.

Victor Paul Wierwille, in his book *Jesus Christ, Our Promised Seed*, uses Scriptural, historical, and astronomical evidence to evaluate and answer the question, "When was Jesus Christ born?" Western Christians traditionally celebrate Christ's birth on December 25. It may be possible that He was conceived at this time, but His birth would have actually occurred in the early Fall, more than likely on or near one of the Fall feasts of Israel.

Scholars have placed Christ's birth from as early as 7 B.C. to as late as 1 B.C. No early church source places the birth of Christ before 4 B.C. In fact, Clement of Alexandria, Tertullian, Julius Africanus, Bishop Hippolytus of Rome, Origen and Euseubus all date the birth of Christ between 3 B.C. and 2 B.C. Also, Josephus records an eclipse that occurred at the death of Herod.

Secular history records five major eclipses from 5 B.C. to January 9, 1 B.C. Jesus was in Egypt at the time Herod died, and the angels told Joseph it was safe to bring Jesus back to Israel (Matthew 2:19-20). Most evidence points to the January 9, 1 B.C. eclipse being the one that occurred at Herod's death. This would coincide with Jesus' birth being either 2 or 3 B.C., since Christ was in Egypt for a brief time as an infant.

The Magi saw "His star." The ancients considered all heavenly bodies as stars, including the planets (except the sun and moon). In ancient history, Jupiter was considered the star of kingship, even among ancient Jewish scholars.

Three years before the birth of Moses, Jupiter and Saturn were in conjunction in the constellation Pisces. Josephus, Abarbanel, Eliazar and other historians affirm that Egyptian astronomers interpreted this sign as an indicator that a great man would be born among the Jews. Perhaps this is why Pharaoh placed heavier workloads on the Hebrews.

What cosmic event happened between 3 and 2 B.C. that would have served as a sign of the birth of the King of the Jews? In both 3 B.C. and 2 B.C., there was a series of conjunctions that involved the planet Jupiter. In 3 B.C. Jupiter, the planet representing King David, was in conjunction with Regulus, the star of kingship, in the constellation Leo the lion, considered to represent the tribe of Judah. This conjunction in the lion would have served as a sign of the birth of a leader.

The Book of Revelation gives the prophetic scene that unfolded at the birth of Christ, and tells us how Satan attempted to kill Christ after His birth:

> And there appeared a great wonder in heaven; a woman clothed with the sun, and the moon under her feet, and upon her head a crown of twelve stars: and she being with child travailing in birth, and pained to be delivered (Revelation 12:1, 2).

The scene is describing in graphic terms the astronomical activity at the time of Christ's birth. Mary, Christ's mother, was a virgin. The constellation Virgo represents a virgin. In Revelation 12, the sun appears to "clothe the woman."

As the sun travels its elliptical trajectory through a year, it enters into the body of the constellation Virgo. The sun is in the area between the neck and the knees, for approximately 24 hours. A new moon is formed during this period under the feet of Virgo.

According to Victor Wierwille, on September 11, 3 B.C., the sun and moon were in such a position in the constellation Virgo. On September 11, sunset was at 6:18 p.m. and moonset at 7:39 p.m. It would have been during this 81-minute period of time that Christ would have been born in Bethlehem, the city of David, of the tribe of Judah! The Gospel of Luke indicates the shepherds visited the child at night. This was Tishri 1 on the Jewish calendar.

September 11, 3 B.C. was also a Jewish feast day known as Rosh Hashanah. This is the Jewish New Year. According to Hebrew tradition, Rosh Hashanah is the time Adam was created. The reckoning of the Chronicles of the king was counted from first Tishri 1, because it was the beginning or head of the year on the Hebrew calendar (*Rosh* means head).

September 11, 3 B.C. is believed by other researchers such as Craig Chester, co-founder of the Monterey Institute for the Research of Astronomy, to be the actual day Christ was born in Bethlehem. Dr. Ernest Martin, in his book *The Star of Bethlehem: the Star that Astonished the World*, also indicates that according to the cosmic signs, the birth of Christ was on September 11, 3 B.C. These books and articles were written years before the attack that shook the world! Those who assume the Bible says little about the importance of cosmic activity should perhaps reconsider their opinions in the light of the Scriptures.

AL-QAEDA AND SEPTEMBER 11

One can be almost certain that Al-Qaeda did not position America's terrorist attack for September 11 as an assault on Christianity because of Christ's birthday. Yet, if this date is correct, it is imaginable that our spiritual adversary selected September 11 as the season for a major strike as a mockery of America, which is globally recognized as a Christian nation.

The prophetic imagery in Revelation 12 is that of a male child being born to rule the nations. It pictures the dragon (Satan) attempting to destroy the child. The man child, who is Christ, is "caught up to the throne of God." Afterwards, Satan sets his attention towards a remnant of believers.

According to Biblical prophecy, the Antichrist and the false prophet will produce their own supernatural signs to impress humanity to follow their diabolical program (see Revelation 13:12-15; 2 Thessalonians 2:9). With such warning, we should not be surprised when strange and unusual signs begin to appear in the Muslim world. After all, the Apostle Paul warned of the danger of spiritual deception inspired by satanic signs and wonders:

> Whose coming is after the working of Satan with all power and signs and lying wonders, and with all deceivableness of unrighteousness in them that perish; because they received not the love of the truth, that they might be saved. And for this cause God shall send them strong delusion, that they should believe a lie (2 Thessalonians 2:9-11).

Often in Scripture and in prophecy, bleeding images, crying statues and other supernatural phenomena are nothing more than an assignment of the Adversary to draw attention away from Christ. They are attempts to draw attention away from the Bible and the truth. The birth of a lamb in a Muslim village helps to illustrate this danger.

MUSLIMS AND THE LAMB OF GOD

Just as Christians carefully discern the signs of the times (Matthew 16:3) to ascertain the prophetic season we are in, Muslims likewise have their own conviction about the last days and the signs that precede the Mahdi and the day of judgment. They, too, believe we live in a momentous season. From time to time, an unusual incident will generate renewed concern in the approaching last days.

Such interest was generated in Uzbekistan with the birth of a lamb. The headlines of *The Nando Times* read "Lamb of God Brings Consolation, Controversy." To a Christian, the title would suggest an article about Jesus Christ whose life of sacrifice identified Him as the "Lamb of God" (John 1:29). Instead, the article told of a lamb that was born in Durmen Village in Uzbekistan.

Born three days before Eid al-Adha, the Islamic holiday marking the end of Muslims' annual pilgrimage to Mecca and Medina in Saudi Arabia, the lamb had unusual white patterns on its black fleece. The patterns resembled the Arabic mark for the word Allah on one side, and the mark for the name Muhammad on the other side.

The markings on the lamb caused a major stir, drawing visitors from China, Turkey, Central Asia and all the Arabic nations. How could a lamb be born with these two marks on its sides? Was this a mere natural phenomenon, a sign from Allah, or the early stages of what the Apostle Paul warned of—signs and wonders that will eventually cause people to be deceived?

THE FINAL SIGNS

Muslims, Jews and Christians believe there are certain signs of the end of the age. The Muslims believe in the Mahdi and various signs of the end of time. The religious Jews are looking for the Messiah and have a series of Old Testament prophecies that indicate the birth pangs of the Messiah have arrived. Christians combine both the Old and New Testament revelations to form a Scriptural end-time theology.

The difference between Christian theology and Islamic beliefs is that, to the Christian, the Bible is a book of prophecy and redemption; while the Koran is a book of simple instruction. The fulfillment of Biblical signs gives ample proof that the Scriptures are true. Cosmic signs are only one part of the evidence that indicates we are in the time of the end.

Fifteen

THE HANDWRITING ON AMERICA'S WALL

They drank wine, and praised the gods of gold, and of silver, of brass, of iron, of wood, and of stone. In the same hour came forth fingers of a man's hand, and wrote over against the candlestick upon the plaster of the wall of the king's palace: and the king saw the part of the hand that wrote. Then the king's countenance was changed, and his thoughts troubled him, so that the joints of his loins were loosed, and his knees smote one against another (Daniel 5:4-6).

No one in the kingdom knew that the party was about to be over. The city of Babylon was the global military and economic headquarters of the ancient world. Fortified with massive walls and protected by a skilled army, it was considered the titanic of cities; it was impregnable! On the fateful night, the best wine in the world was being drunk from gold chalices. The banquet hall alone was a mile long and over 1,600 feet wide. Lining the walls were huge carved elephants with polished bronze gladiators positioned on their shoulders, silently overlooking the activities.

From a golden chain draped from post to post hung thousands of flowers, filling the hall with a natural perfume. In the corner of the hall an orchestra of 35,000 trained musicians entertained. The banquet tables were shaped like horseshoes, and trained peacocks pulled miniature chariots carrying the wine and cheese from table to table. This, according to C. M. Ward, former radio speaker for the Assemblies of God, was the setting in Babylon the night God crashed the king's party.

Within seconds, the drunken revelry came to a screeching halt. The thunderous noise of laughing was silenced as a massive hand appeared against the plaster of the banquet hall and began writing the words, "You are weighed in the balance and found wanting. Your kingdom will be divided between the Medes and Persians."

The drunken king was unaware that an invading army was sneaking through an underground tunnel and would soon make its move. Before the sun rose in the morning, the city of Babylon would be under the control of the Medes and Persians. The overthrow of Babylon happened within 24 hours. No leader saw it coming except for a prophet named Daniel who could interpret the handwriting on the wall!

Sudden Changes Within 24 Hours

On September 10, several men were sitting in a bar in Tampa, Florida. All were of Middle Eastern descent. They were overheard telling each other, "Tomorrow America will get it. New York and Washington will have their day." Those near them assumed they had too much to drink and ignored their comments.

In Baton Rouge, Louisiana, a young Muslim man had pressed a young Christian woman to marry him and she refused. Shortly before September 11, he called her to tell her he could not give an explanation, but was on his way to New Jersey and would have to leave the car in the parking lot of the church she attended. On September 11, he was missing and the car was in the parking lot. Weeks later, he returned without any explanation.

Before sunrise on the morning of September 11, something strange was happening. A local pastor in a northeastern city observed something he had never seen before. He knew that Friday was the Muslim holy day, and the mosque near his home was always filled with people at that time. But why was there so much activity this early on a Tuesday morning? Cars were at the mosque, and a meeting was going on.

The pastor had never seen this before. He felt something strange was up, but had no clue about what it could be. Apparently, those attending the mosque knew something was coming within a few hours.

A man who attends a large Assembly of God in Florida was returning home from a business trip. He had a long layover in Boston's Logan International Airport, and would board an early flight back to Pensacola the next day. Sitting alone at his gate in the early hours of the morning, he observed a young Middle Eastern woman sitting alone with a purse and a cell phone. From her seat, she could see the airport tower. She was continually making calls, and peering back and forth at the tower and the runway.

Long before most of the passengers arrived at the gate, three men wearing the same kind of shirt with a travel company logo approached the woman. He heard one say, "How long must you stay here?" She replied, "Just a little longer." The men spoke Arabic then left. Moments later, she exited the area and was not seen again. A few hours later, after arriving in Pensacola, he heard of airplanes taking off from Logan airport and attacking the Twin Towers. He reported the information and was convinced the woman and the three men were part of the plan. A Florida paper originally reported the incident, but then the report was dropped.

I first heard this information I am now telling you from a woman who lives in Florida near the school where President Bush spoke on September 11. That morning, a white van with two Middle Eastern-looking men pulled up to the school. There appeared to be television cameras in the van. They informed the security personnel that they were a television crew, and had a scheduled meeting with President Bush following his speech. They wanted to set up the equipment for the interview.

The security personnel checked with the Secret Service, who forbade the men from entering because there was no record of them or any pre-authorized interview. Upon hearing this, the men drove away from the school. As they were driving away from the school, an eyewitness saw the men in the van shake their fists out the window and scream something about death to America and Bush. The van fled away and hours later, the president was whisked away from the school to an underground bunker for protection.

Only days before, in Afghanistan, the head of the Afghan Northern Alliance had been killed by men posing as journalists who had cameras filled with deadly explosives. It may have been possible that these two men were terrorists who believed they could perform the same function by taking out the President at the same time the towers were falling. Of course this would have been carried out on television as the cameras were rolling.

On September 10, life was going as usual with no national interruptions. Planes were filled with travelers, children were sitting at their desks in schools and 50,000 people in and around the Twin Towers in New York City were conducting routine global business. Within 24 hours, the handwriting was on the wall, and from place to place strange warning signs could be seen but nobody could decipher them.

Bin Laden had announced in June of 2001, that he would hit America within two weeks. The date he had set was July 4, America's Day of Independence. When July 4 passed without incident, nobody paid much attention to the handwriting that continued to appear on the wall.

SECRETS IN THE MOSQUE

We know in retrospect that certain Muslims throughout the world had knowledge that an attack was being planned against America. One story told of a Jewish family in New York that had become friends with a Muslim family across the street.

The Muslim businessman warned the Jewish friend not to be in downtown New York City anytime on September 11. He told him he could not give details, but to please not go into New York City. On the morning of September 11, the Jewish man noticed that his neighbor's house was empty. Apparently, the family moved out in the middle of the night and has not been heard from since.

Behind the doors of Islamic mosques, Muslims with Middle Eastern and Asian connections heard whispers from fellow worshipers that an attack was being planned against the United States. They may not have known the details, but some knew it was coming.

Months before the attack, a Jewish friend residing in Florida was in the same flight school where one of the hijackers was being trained to fly a plane. My friend actually met one of the men and recognized that there was something suspicious about him. When he saw the pictures on television of the 19 hijackers, he reported his information to intelligence agencies in Washington, D.C.

Mounting evidence indicates that several agencies received vague warnings prior to the attack, but the handwriting on the wall was covered by the red tape of bureaucracy.

Such ignorance of the facts was apparent when one U.S. government agency released the visas for two of the hijackers months after they had already enacted their plot and died on the planes they hijacked.

WHAT THE RUSSIANS KNEW

In July of 2001, Dr. Tatyana Koryagina, a senior research fellow at the Institute of Macroeconomic Research, made a prediction that America would experience a financial attack. Her article, published in *Pravda*, was titled, "The Dollar and America Will Fall Down on August 19." She was quoted as saying:

> The U.S. has been chosen as the object of financial attack because the financial center of the planet is located there. The effect will be maximal. The strike waves of economic crisis will spread over the planet instantly, and will remind us of the blast of a huge nuclear bomb.

According to Koryagina, the individuals behind the attacks were not the 19 terrorists, but a group of men seeking to reshape the world. She claims this is an extremely powerful group of private individuals with total assets of about $300 trillion dollars. They wish to legalize their power and form a new world government.

Dr. Korygina predicted that the terrorists will again "strike America in the back" and bring it down. The purpose is to destroy America as the world's number one economy and make room for a group of elite, wealthy persons to eventually control the world through their personal wealth and power.

Before a person writes off her predictions, remember the Scriptures predict the formation of a seventh and eighth empire. The seventh empire will rule for a short time, followed by the eighth empire that will trample the nations through the Antichrist leadership (Revelation 17:10-12). In the time of the end, 10 kings (countries) will give their kingdoms over to the Antichrist. At some point, the 10 kings and the final empires of prophecy must form.

Biblical scholars note that the prophetic writers speak of the east, south, and north, but the west appears to be missing. Many of the end time prophecies will be fulfilled around the Middle East, Europe and Asia. The West may be missing because we have come under a devastating attack, or because we are consumed with our own internal difficulties. At some point, the globalists will succeed and an Islamic leader will wait in the wings until it is time to make his move. Therefore, the doctor's information has credibility.

The question is, how could someone in Russia predict such economic attacks and compare them to the "blast of a huge nuclear bomb" two months before the event? Was the doctor previously informed or was it coincidence? She is said to be in Putin's inner circle.

Intelligence reports indicate that the Russian mafia has, for some time, been selling supplies, including components for chemical, biological and nuclear weapons, to Osama bin Laden and his al-Qaida network. In the past, Russia has supported some of the world's worst terrorist nations, including Iran, Libya and North Korea.

The sale of weapons and components was part of the al-Qaeda operation in Afghanistan. The Taliban would grow poppy plants, the seeds of which are used to produce heroin. The seeds were sold to the Russian mafia on the black market in return for weapons, weapon building information and raw materials to successfully wage a terrorist campaign.

The dangerous aspect of such an alignment is the possibility of chemical, biological and nuclear weapons being unleased upon a major American city. Knowing this threat, the United States federal government is preparing vaccines and suggesting that cities have contingency plans in the event of such an emergency.

SHOULD WE HAVE KNOWN IN ADVANCE?

One of the issues that will undoubtedly be debated for years to come is whether America's vast and expensive intelligence network was asleep at the wheel in the weeks and months leading up to the September 11 attacks. Critics have questioned how a conspiracy to seize four large commercial jetliners and use them for guided missiles could go undetected.

Some in the intelligence community argue, perhaps rightfully so, that suicide missions of any kind are virtually impossible to stop. According to a Reuters News Service report, dated July 11, 2001, Asst. Director Dale Watson of the FBI's Counter-Terrorism Division told a National Governors Association Conference:

> We predict major terrorist attacks against U.S. interests overseas, one per year for the next five years. I'm not a gloom-and-doom type person, but I will tell you what I see and what most smart people see: The United States is headed for an incident inside the United States.

To those operatives in the intelligence field, it has never been a matter of *if*, but only a matter of *when*. That is, they knew that eventually terrorists would strike at the U.S. within our borders. The best to be hoped for was to keep tabs on the people who were considered a threat and do everything possible to thwart their attempts. Obviously, on September 11 those efforts failed. To be fair, however, we should say that if someone has made up their mind to die a martyr and take as many with them as possible, little can be done.

The fact is, not only have we been expecting such an attack, but we have also known from where it would most likely originate—fundamentalist Islam. For close to 30 years, people have been warning about the expansion of militant Islam and what that portends for the West and, specifically, the United States. We saw the transformation that took place in Iran during the late 70s and early 80s, and apparently assumed it could be contained. A decade later, the West waged a war against a despot in the very cradle of Islam, but saw fit to leave him in power.

We know that there have been close calls with Islamic operatives in the past few years within our own borders. Of course, the closest call we know of was the first bombing of the World Trade Center in New York. It is still baffling how the bomb did no more damage than it did. We also know that in the days just before January 1, 2000, at least two Islamic operatives were stopped at two different gateways into the nation. At least one of those stopped was presumed to be the key to a ring of terrorists operating within the U.S. Yet, despite all this and countless acts of Islamic terror, few Americans took the time to understand the teachings of Islam or appreciate the deadly menace growing among Muhammad's most devout followers. Only in the aftermath of 9/11 did the average American hear so much about Islam, and what they heard was questionable at the least.

There have been other warnings throughout the years that emanated, not from governmental agencies, but from pulpits across America and the world. For at least the past 25 years, Dave Wilkerson has been warning Americans that soon God would allow tragedy to shake this nation. In one book, he described how the city of New York would be in flames. Many other men and women of God have described visions or dreams in which New York was under attack and in flames.

Whether the attacks of September 11 are the fulfillment of these visions is debatable, but to say that America wasn't warned would be false. The Scripture declares that, "Surely the Lord God will do nothing, but he revealeth his secret unto his servants the prophets" (Amos 3:7). This should not be interpreted to mean that God initiated the attacks, but that through His watchmen He has been warning this nation that we have been found wanting on the scales of His justice.

In the Summer of 1999, my good friend, Joe Van Koevering, was in New York to tape some programs for "God's News Behind The News." One of the filming locations was the riverbank opposite Manhattan's skyline. Joe and the crew were attempting to tape, but without much success.

Finally, at the end of an attempted taping, a plane flew directly overhead, creating such a noise that using the film was impossible. The footage was considered to be insignificant and useless . . . that is, until it resurfaced just days after the 9/11 attacks! Then it sent chills through everyone who viewed it.

As Joe stood on the banks of the Hudson River, the towers of the World Trade Center loomed notably over his shoulders. At the climax of his comments, Joe lifted his hand, unaware of the fact that his finger was pointing directly at the pinnacle of the towers. Just as he said that God would "cast down" the false gods of America, Joe's hand came down, almost tracing the same deadly path those towers would take to destruction.

Was it a coincidence, or an eerie hint at what would happen some two years later? Could it be that God wanted to warn us of what would lie ahead?

What the Bible Foresaw

If we as believers accept that God is in control of human history, then we must accept that God allowed the events of that day to unfold. If this is true, we must ask the question "Why?"

I am convinced that God is trying to dispatch a message, not just to the leaders and rank-and-file of our nation, but specifically to the body of believers in America. He is trying to get our attention. Furthermore, I believe there is Biblical evidence of what the Lord is saying to this nation and to the nations of the world through the tragedy and ramifications of 9/11.

Soon after the attacks my friend, Bill Cloud, pointed out to me that there was, within the Bible, a passage with 9/11 overtones. After reading the entire passage (Isaiah 30:1-25) I was persuaded that September 11, 2001, was a dramatic wake-up call for America and for the church. Beyond that, it was an invitation to look more closely at the political and cultural trends in our society and, possibly, a foreshadowing of Islam's role in the end times. Furthermore, a considerable portion of Isaiah 30 can be viewed prophetically; and I believe it actually points to 9/11 as a key element in understanding how the end of the age may unfold.

FOR THE TIME TO COME

Understand, first of all, that some passages of prophetic Scripture can be interpreted as having dual applications. For instance, the Lord identifies Israel in Hosea 11:1 as His son whom He calls "out of Egypt"—referring obviously to Israel's exodus from the land of the Pharaohs. Yet, we see that Matthew quotes this passage when referring to the return of Joseph, Mary and the baby Jesus from Egypt following Herod's death (Matthew 2:15). Thus, some prophetic passages may apply to more than one situation.

With this in mind, certain key passages in Isaiah 30 take on very alarming ramifications. For our purposes, the story should really begin in Isaiah 30:8. The prophet is told, "Now go, write it before them in a table, and note it in a book, that it may be for the time to come for ever and ever." In the Hebrew text, the phrase, "time to come" is *yom acharon*, literally meaning "the last day." When Bill brought this to my attention, I was reminded of when he and I were working on another project in which this Hebrew word *acharon* showed up.

The word *acharon* is very interesting because it is used in other key prophetic passages which speak of the last generation (Psalms 78:4,6; 102:18) Thus, verse 8 strongly infers that the message Isaiah was to receive from God contains a message for the last day —this generation.

As the chapter continues, God accuses Israel of trusting in people and idols rather than in Him. They had taken to themselves strange gods, and had told their spiritual teachers to "prophesy not unto us right things, speak unto us smooth things" (Isaiah 30:10). In other words, Israel succumbed to the same temptation that Paul predicted would seduce a portion of the end-time church: "For the time will come when they will not endure sound doctrine; but after their own lusts shall they heap to themselves teachers, having itching ears" (2 Timothy 4:3).

Longsuffering though He may be, God finally allowed adversity to overtake Israel, no doubt, so that they would acknowledge their sins and turn back to Him. After adversity had visited them, we learn that they turned away from their false gods and destroyed their idols of silver and gold. They called their teachers and the prophets, who they had previously told to speak pleasant things, out of the corner. The teachers in turn told them how they should walk.

In short, spiritual renewal swept across the nation. But we shouldn't miss this important fact. It seems the entire process—the state of the nation, the adversity and subsequent restoration—is defined by Isaiah 30:25 "And there shall be upon every high mountain, and upon every high hill, rivers and streams of waters in the day of the great slaughter, *when the towers fall.*" This verse seems to indicate that Israel's adversity and eventual restoration was initiated by "the day of the great slaughter," a day when towers fell to the ground. In the midst of our tragedy, God was speaking to this nation and to His people through this particular passage of Scripture. In Isaiah's prophecy God wanted the last days generation to take note of the fact that He was warning them. It was as though the handwriting was on the wall. But, as you will see, the ramifications of 9/11 are far greater than many have imagined.

SHOCK AND DISBELIEF

You could see the look of complete surprise and genuine concern come across the face of our Commander-in-Chief when Chief of Staff Andrew Card informed him that the second tower had been deliberately struck by another hijacked airliner. Still, Mr. Bush continued to appear attentive and impressed as the Florida school children he had come to visit continued to read aloud for the President.

But soon after being alerted, the urgency of the situation commandeered his morning schedule. He politely excused himself, made a brief statement to the press and was whisked away to Air Force One to be flown to an undisclosed location. By this time there were rumors that the terrorists knew how to find the President, even if he was aboard the flying White House. No one wanted to take a chance those rumors were true, and so an immediate return to Washington was out of the question.

From the Chief Executive to the teenager flipping hamburgers, it was obvious that everyone was caught off guard and was uncertain of what was going to happen next. Why were we caught off guard? Because this is America! Things like this don't happen here . . . but they did that day. It seemed that God had ordained it!

Americans have long believed that this "nation under God" was protected from foreign invaders. Even after Pearl Harbor was attacked, no one seriously considered the continental United States under threat. And whether all generations of Americans have acknowledged it or not, the true reason we have felt this comfortable and secure is because throughout our history, God has, without fail, intervened on our behalf.

From the moment the first Pilgrims disembarked from the Mayflower, it was obvious that great things were destined for this nation under the watchful eye of a sovereign God. During the Revolution, when there were so many opportunities for the British to annihilate the ragtag Continental Army and squelch the Revolution, the colonists watched in awe as God granted them a way to escape in order to fight another day.

Our forefathers acknowledged that God was guiding their steps and bringing them to the point of being an independent nation. In return they strove to be faithful to Him by insuring that future generations would enjoy the same freedoms they held dear. They established a nation whose laws and values were based upon the greatest of all guides, the Bible.

Throughout our history, the God of Israel has continually watched over this nation through prosperity, distress and uncertainty. Consequently, America has grown accustomed to this security and abundance, to the degree of taking it for granted. So, when it seemed that God permitted something so tragic to occur, we couldn't help but wonder why.

Why Were We Attacked?

I believe there is one basic reason why this tragedy happened. It is described in one word: *relationship*! I am referring to the relationship this nation has enjoyed with God. The fact that this relationship is strained, at best, lies at the root of why we came under attack. Obviously, by permitting the September 11 attacks to be carried out, the Lord is trying to draw our attention to the fact that we have placed this relationship in jeopardy.

He is desirous that we repent and return to Him. "As many as I love, I rebuke and chasten: be zealous therefore, and repent." (Revelation 3:19).

THE SPIRIT OF ANTICHRIST IN AMERICA

In the days just after the 9/11 attacks it seemed that there was a desire among Americans to turn back to the Lord. But just when you began to be hopeful that spiritual renewal was beginning to sweep the land, the liberals and atheists came out eager to negate any acknowledgment of reverence and need for God.

One example of this was the decision by an Appeals Court in San Francisco that ruled that schoolchildren should not recite the pledge of allegiance because the phrase "under God" violates the First Amendment. When the decision was met with protest from almost every politician in Washington—not to mention millions of average citizens—the Court said it would "reconsider."

The ruling came on a complaint filed by a California atheist on behalf of his daughter. It seems she did not personally have a problem with the pledge; yet, the father felt it was treacherous for teachers to compel his daughter to recite this phrase "against her will." In an interview with FOX News' Tony Snow, it became evident that the plaintiff's objection was not with the reference to "God" but the inference that "under God" actually meant "under Jesus."

In other words, his problem was with acknowledging the Son of God as the spiritual guardian and savior of our nation. He denied the very notion that Jesus is the Son of God; and that is, by definition, the spirit of antichrist. The Apostle John warned that, "Every spirit that confesseth not that Jesus Christ is come in the flesh is not of God: and this is that spirit of antichrist, whereof ye have heard that it should come; and even now already is it in the world" (I John 4:3). Therefore, as asinine as this Court decision was, we really shouldn't be surprised by it or its timing. America is still recovering from one of its most tragic times, and many Americans are wondering how the God of the Bible factors into this.

Even so, in spite of the severity of our national crisis, those who are offended by the message of the Bible will not cease their attempts to remove that message from our classrooms and city halls. It is absolutely amazing that atheism has been so successful in rewriting the history of America. By and large, they have convinced Americans that this nation's founders never wanted God and politics to share the same space. Yet, as we have already noted, America's founding fathers acknowledged that this nation was indebted to God on a colossal scale. They understood the only way to honor the debt was to honor Him as our Sovereign Protector, to adopt the principles of His Word as the basis of our society and to make His laws the law of the land. George Washington is quoted as saying,

> No people can be bound to acknowledge and adore the Invisible Hand, which conducts the affairs of men more than the people of the United States. Every step by which they have advanced to the character of an independent nation seems to have been distinguished by some token of providential agency. . . . We ought to be no less persuaded that the propitious smiles of Heaven can never be expected on a nation that disregards the eternal rules of order and right which Heaven itself has ordained.

Mr. Washington not only confirms that the founders acknowledged the United States as being founded providentially. He also warned future generations that should we disregard what God ordains, then those blessings we hold so dear—liberty, abundance and so forth—may one day cease to be available to us. September 11 could be a dramatic indication that this possibility may already be upon us. Did God allow those towers to fall so that His people would be directed to Isaiah 30 and learn from its lessons?

BLESSINGS AND CURSES

In my book *Plucking The Eagle's Wings*, I compare the amazing prophetic parallels between the ancient nation of Israel and the founding of America. I noted that the same blessings promised to Israel are the same blessings experienced in America, but the same curses that were released for Israel's sins are also the same problems that America is beginning to experience.

This is because both nations, Israel and America, are founded and built upon a spiritual covenant with God, and the Bible is the source of their moral laws and the foundation of both nation's spiritual constitutions.

Israel's blessings were contingent upon their full obedience to the Word of God. If they lived free from sin and walked in the commandments of God, then blessings would follow their nation and impact their families:

> And it shall come to pass, if thou shalt hearken diligently unto the voice of the Lord thy God, to observe and to do all his commandments which I command thee this day, that the Lord thy God will set thee on high above all nations of the earth. All these blessings shall come on thee, and overtake thee, if thou shalt hearken unto the voice of the Lord thy God.
>
> Blessed shalt thou be in the city, and blessed shalt thou be in the field. Blessed shall be the fruit of thy body, and the fruit of thy ground, and the fruit of thy cattle, the increase of thy kine, and the flocks of thy sheep. Blessed shall be thy basket and thy store. Blessed shalt thou be when thou comest in, and blessed shalt thou be when thou goest out (Deuteronomy 28:1-6).

We also see that if Israel failed to obey the laws of God and sinned against the covenant—worshiped idols, committed adultery and mistreated their fellow man—then God, in order to bring them to humility and repentance, would lift the favor and the blessing and allow great trouble and distress to strike the nation.

> And I will bring a sword upon you, that shall avenge the quarrel of my covenant: and when ye are gathered together within your cities, I will send the pestilence among you; and ye shall be delivered into the hand of the enemy (Leviticus 26:25).

God instructed Israel that one of the first manifestations of His judgment upon the nation would be they would experience "terror."

> I also will do this unto you; I will even appoint over you terror (Leviticus 26:16).

> The sword without, and terror within, shall destroy both the young man and the virgin, the suckling also with the man of gray hairs (Deuteronomy 32:25).

America has fought several wars on our own soil, including the Revolution and the Civil War. Never in our young history have we fought a war with such a small group of people (19 hijackers) whose actions impacted the economy and increased the fear factor so quickly. It was as though the Almighty allowed a protective hedge to be lifted for a brief period of time, to say to America, "Here is what can happen if I am not protecting you."

THE PENALTY FOR SHEDDING INNOCENT BLOOD?

Sooner or later America had to answer for some of our choices. This is not to say that the deaths of over 3,000 people is in some way compensation for past mistakes, but yet many people felt the nation was on a collision course with tragedy. We have known for years that an accounting would have to be given for the innocent blood shed over the years as a result of abortion. This is especially true in light of what has happened since it was legalized by Roe vs. Wade in 1973.

Years ago on a tour to the Holy Land, I visited the ancient site of Jericho. While the tour group looked upon the heap of stones that used to be a city, our guide, Gideon Shor, said that within the crumbled walls of the ancient city, the remains of infant children had been found. He didn't mean that these infants had been buried beneath the collapse. He meant that the remains had been found within the bricks themselves.

In essence, the Canaanites had literally built the walls of their cities with the bones of children sacrificed to pagan gods. When God caused the walls to fall, it was if to say, He would not allow a civilization to stand that would do that to children. Just think of it—in one day the ancient walls and presumably towers of Jericho fell flat, destroying all those who had looked to those walls as complete security.

On September 11, was God sending a message to this nation that to kill over 40 million innocent babies since January 1973 (according to National Right To Life statistics) under the guise of women's rights merits severe consequences? Furthermore, the argument could be made that to those who perform abortions, it is not an issue of pro-life or pro-choice; it is strictly a matter of money, a matter of economic stability. Unfortunately for America, it is the potential economic effect that decides many of the moral issues that trouble us in America today.

Thus, those towers were not only a symbol of our financial might, but memorials to the many times we said "No" to what was right in favor of the fast buck. In Babylon, the handwriting appeared upon the palace wall. In America, the handwriting was on our wall—Wall Street.

Time to Face the Music

It is time for us all to be realistic. Instead of a display of gratitude to the One who has blessed this nation with freedom, our arrogance has driven us to defy Him in an effort to be free from Him. Instead of showing our thankfulness for the blessings He has bestowed upon us, our response has been to worship the blessing instead. Considering the unique history of our nation, our relationship with God and understanding how the Lord deals with those He loves, September 11 was bound to happen. The handwriting was on the wall!

Just days after the September 11 tragedy, *TIME* published a special edition devoted totally to the events of that day. In that edition one reporter wrote:

> If you want to humble an empire it makes sense to maim its cathedrals. They are symbols of its faith, and when they crumple and burn, it tells us we are not so powerful and we can't be safe. The Twin Towers of the World Trade Center, planted at the base of Manhattan island with the Stature of Liberty as their sentry, and the Pentagon, a squat, concrete fort on the banks of the Potomac, are the sanctuaries of money and power that our enemies may imagine define us. But that assumes our faith rests on what we can buy and build, and that has never been America's true God.

Had this been written two hundred years ago, it would have been much more accurate. In the infancy of our nation, we depended on God. However, what once was certain has since become a question mark. Perhaps our gods *are* currently personified in these two buildings, and that is exactly why these two landmarks were struck with such ferocity. Maybe our gods are the very abilities and ingenuity that designed and constructed those concrete icons. Is it not our immense diversity and collective capability that we take so much pride in? Is this not what we uphold as the *true* "Spirit of America"?

In this day and age, it might be accurate to say that the United States has become a nation "under many gods." With the influx of so many different nationalities and religions, America the melting pot might one day become America the boiling pot. Should we fail to respond to the warnings of 9/11 in the manner Israel responded to the day of great slaughter (Isaiah. 30:25), similar dramatic events will continue to occur.

IN 24 HOURS, AMERICA WAS CHANGED

Within 24 hours, New York City and America were changed forever. Since New York City is considered the economic capital of the world, it would be a prime target for those wanting to tear the economic structure of the nation into shreds. Former Prime Minister of Israel Benjamin Netanyahu said, "America received a wake-up call from hell."

He and others have pointed out that Brooklyn is home to 2.5 million Jews, and that it houses the largest Jewish population of any single city in the world. He, along with others, believes that in a matter of time, New York City will be assaulted with nuclear weapons. It is only a matter of time before terrorists have and are willing to use such weapons.

Missionary Kelvin McDaniel ministered recently in Indonesia, the country with the largest Muslim population in the world. While ministering on a main island, he was told by a pastor's wife that the al-Qaeda organization was active on their island, and they believed that worldwide jihad had come. She told Kelvin, "Without a doubt, they want to destroy the United States."

One evening while traveling through the jungle, the pastor saw several Western troops who were camouflaged, with moss attached to their outer garments. These Special Forces are collecting vital information. The problem is, there are more radicals in the world than there are Special Forces.

No doubt the two top cities being targeted for future strikes are New York and Washington D.C. New York is the economic center, the headquarters for the United Nations, and the home of millions of Jews. Washington, D.C. is the nation's capital, and also contains the historic symbolism and government buildings that keep the nation on course.

According to sources inside of Israel, many religious Jews in New York City are looking into the possibility of leaving America if another major attack hits close to their home. Mr. Sharon announced in 2001 his plan to see over one million Jews return to Israel. The Bible predicts that just prior to the return of the Lord, the Jews will return to Israel from the north, the south, the east and the west (see Jeremiah 16:15, 16, Zechariah 8:7, Isaiah 49:6-12).

Presently, Jews have returned from three of the four areas. In the future, they will return from the west, perhaps only after a large city, such as New York City, has experienced its greatest terrorist attack in history. Mr. Sharon may get his wishes in a few months or years if we see a major assault on one or more cities with major Jewish populations.

WHAT COULD HAVE HAPPENED

The sad picture of a gaping pit in New York will be a visual reminder of what happened on that fateful September morning. But let us be thankful for what did not happen. According to my sources, it is believed that a total of 12 planes were targeted for hijacking on September 11. Four were in the sky and the others never made it off the ground. After the passengers were released from the planes, some of the would-be terrorists left the terminals and other suspects were later interrogated.

Suspected strikes may have been planned for the Sears Tower in Chicago, the Space Needle in Seattle, the Centers for Disease Control in Atlanta and a chemical plant in Louisiana. The plane that crashed in Pennsylvania was at first believed to be heading toward the Capitol, but the actual destination appears to have been the White House. This ambush by Islamic radicals could have been far worse than it was.

WHAT DOES THE FUTURE HOLD?

In October of 2001 I received a phone call from a retired military Colonel. Our weekly television program aired a series of specials from Israel, including one in front of a tank in the Golan Heights, and the second a teaching series in front of the Eastern Gate in Jerusalem. The information released on our program created quite a stir among some Israelis and Muslims. I was informed that a group of Muslims had viewed a particular program on satellite and were making copies of the teaching, distributing them into several Islamic nations. It appears I had shared information about Israel's military and certain Muslims were very interested in these facts.

Several noted individuals had asked this man to contact me with this information. Eventually, our conversation turned from my television programs to Islamic terrorists. I was expressing my opinion that America would be struck by Islamic radicals in the future. The Colonel not only agreed but added an observation. Based on his personal knowledge and evidence from intelligence sources, he was convinced that terrorists would strike with a biological or chemical attack in a major city or at a major event where a large number of people were gathered. He said it was *"not a matter of if, but a matter of when."* The Colonel believed it was possible for literally hundreds of thousands of people to be killed at one time with countless numbers severely injured.

The possibility for a massive terrorist attack is now so great that some Americans live with an apprehension of the future. This may be what Jesus alluded to when he predicted:

Men's hearts failing them for fear, and for looking after those
things which are coming to pass upon the earth (Luke 21:26).

The rise in heart failure would be a result of what *will be*
coming to pass and not what *has previously* occurred. Small
pox, anthrax, Ebola, mustard gas, and nuclear weapons are
words that create mental images of violent suffering, panic
and sudden death. Each of these items can presently be made
into weapons used to strike the nation.

When God allowed the ungodly masses to be punished
in Noah's day, He unleashed a huge volume of water, a
universal flood. When he permitted the destruction of Sodom
and Gomorrah, fire and brimstone from an underground
explosion near the Dead Sea became the "weapon." Both
times Jerusalem fell into the hands of her enemies, the
city was consumed with fire.

Again, the question is not will America be hit again, but
what will we do the next time? The Sunday following September 11th, church attendance was up 30 percent. Three
months later, it was back to normal and about 8 months
later, it was a little below average. Perhaps Americans were
confused. The nation became patriotic, but did not repent
of the sins of murder, abortion, addictions and unbelief.
The rise in patriotism caused a "feel-good goose-bump" sensation to warm the hearts of Americans. Yet, we may have
missed the point. A few blocks from the Trade Center and the
New York Stock Exchange sits a brass bull. For seven straight
years the "bull market" took charge as money was made,
almost without effort. But people continued to sin.

The enemies of America will strike in our homeland again.
In fact, there will be a series of strikes spaced over a period
of time that will impact our nation. This is why it is important for our national leaders to be men and women of faith.
We must have leaders who are not ashamed to seek God
and ask for the nation to pray. Our hope as a nation of people
lies in the blessed promise God gave to Israel:

> If my people, which are called by my name, shall humble themselves, and pray, and seek my face, and turn from their wicked ways; then will I hear from heaven, and will forgive their sin, and will heal their land (2 Chronicles 7:14).

It is the responsibility of those who have a covenant with God to stand in the gap and repent for the sins of the nation. God said, "If *My* people," not "If sinners." Terror attacks can be thwarted and evil plans exposed through prayer. Throughout history, God has established a place of refuge in times of adversity. America has been blessed to be a safe haven and our enemies despise this. Yet, as we saw on September 11, that "safe haven" became a dangerous and uncertain place. Scripture seems to have implied that long ago.

God saw that this generation would be affected by a day of great slaughter when the towers fell, and sought to warn His people of national *and* global ramifications. You see, Isaiah's prophecy in chapter 30 seems to hint that the day of great slaughter is simply the opening scene in the final act of world history.

Thus, the handwriting on America's wall serves as a warning for the entire world of what is to come.

Sixteen

So What Can America Do?

When thou art in tribulation, and all these things are come upon thee, even in the latter days, if thou turn to the Lord thy God, and shalt be obedient unto his voice; (for the Lord thy God is a merciful God;) he will not forsake thee, neither destroy thee, nor forget the covenant of thy fathers which he sware unto them (Deuteronomy 4:30, 31).

THE UNTOUCHABLES

Do you remember the old television program, "The Untouchables?" It was a program about Elliot Ness and his team of formidable "G-Men." Because they could not be tainted with the corruption that ran rampant in Chicago law enforcement during the Depression Era, they were dubbed "Untouchable."

Although these brave men could ward off bribes from the Mob, unfortunately some of them were unable to meet with the same success when it came to the Mob's bullets. No one is untouchable!

For many years, Americans have felt that we were untouchable. No doubt this false sense of security was fostered by our lavish and relatively peaceful lifestyles. Complacency, like a deadly disease, runs rampant throughout our society, dulling the senses and distorting conventional wisdom. When trends and developments in the world demand that we take notice and act accordingly, complacency pushes the warning aside and convinces us that everything is alright.

Even more than the diabolical schemes of those who are resolved to conquer the weaker, complacency has served the god of war unlike no other servant. Throughout history, it has often proved to be what the war-monger was dependent on in order for his battle plans to succeed.

Take, for example, the Munich Pact of September 1938. This agreement, signed by Germany, Italy, France and Great Britain, was an attempt to appease Hitler's territorial demands in Czechoslovakia. When British Prime Minister Neville Chamberlain returned home from the summit meeting, he declared "peace in our time." In March 1939, however, Germany occupied the remainder of the country and invaded Poland in September 1939, officially launching World War II.

Thus history teaches, and personal experience confirms, that whether on an individual or national scale, human nature too often requires tragedy in order to awaken people to reality. A false sense of security can be lethal to a nation and to a person.

So many are procrastinators by nature and never do what should have been done until crisis dictates that it must. Those with a tendency to postpone are typically motivated solely by crisis and calamity. Unfortunately, these prerequisite emergencies often result in death—

sometimes spiritual, many times literal. When it comes to spiritual matters, some hard-headed individuals continue to tread the rebellious path even in the face of tribulation.

To some degree, America has changed for the better since September 2001. Yet, it is distressing to see that mainstream America has once again reverted to a false sense of security. The typical American is not overly concerned about the threats that face us around the world. We don't travel abroad as much and we tend to be a bit more anxious about flying, but for the most part, life has not changed that much in America.

Once again, our luxuries have successfully seduced us into thinking that 9-11 was an isolated event. Despite the government's attempt to keep everyone on their toes, most Americans have been deluded into thinking that we are relatively safe from enemies abroad and from within. Therefore, it seems that it is only a matter of time before, once again, some type of national disaster strikes.

One good thing that can be said about adversity is that it typically unites people for a common good. Furthermore, in America's history, adversity has almost always caused the leaders and the populace to reflect upon the spiritual condition of the nation and to repent when transgressions are revealed. Thus, it seems safe to say that God has *allowed* national calamities to serve the purpose of bringing about national repentance.

Still, a lingering fear is that 21st century America is less likely to repent of her ways in the face of such adversity. I have often said that, "America knows how to pray, but has forgotten how to repent." This is sad but true.

Scripture reveals that a day is coming when, in spite of disastrous events, man will not repent of his transgressions (Revelation 9:20, 21). Instead of softening their hearts, different plagues will have the opposite effect—men will harden their hearts toward God. Is it possible that this has, in some degree, already taken place in America?

Furthermore, could it be that wealth and a false sense of security accentuates the dilemma? When circumstances interrupt our lifestyles, mankind has the tendency to resent and reject the one they think could have or should have prevented their little world from being upset. Often God receives the hate mail.

It would be nice to say that the church is exempt from this kind of thinking, but it is not. In fact, there are elements within the church that plant, water and nourish the notion that Christians are untouchable. We are led to believe by some that bad things shouldn't happen to those who are believers.

While we do believe that our relationship with God does protect us from evil and attacks from the enemy, we do not believe that we are exempt from adversity. It is adversity that, in fact, allows us the opportunity to grow into a complete and mature Christian (James 1:2-4). Yet, many feel that when they are in the midst of adversity, it is simply an attempt to hinder them or that somehow God is not doing His job.

Akin to this "untouchable" concept is the idea that believers should be wealthy, not because they work for it or practice biblical principles, but *just because*! While God wants us to prosper (3 John 1:2), He will not bless those who conform to unwise, unethical and unscriptural principles. Wealth in the hands of those who are immature can have disastrous consequences, namely that they are seduced into thinking that the presence of wealth constitutes approval of their lifestyle.

Furthermore, people with wealth typically want more wealth, and human nature is such that we begin focusing on the blessings rather than on the One who provides the

blessings. Sooner or later, wealth in the hands of those immature and unprepared for the tests that will surely follow
are overcome with cares and heavy burdens. Jesus said,

> And take heed to yourselves, lest at any time your hearts
> be overcharged with surfeiting, and drunkenness, and cares
> of this life, and so that day come upon you unawares. For
> as a snare shall it come on all them that dwell on the face
> of the whole earth (Luke 21:34, 35).

In essence, He warns us not to let our guard down and
allow spiritually unhealthy attitudes and deeds become
part of our life. He advises us not to conform to a false
sense of security and be lulled into spiritual slumber. If
we do, the consequences could be overwhelming.

Again, as believers, we have a heavenly Father who
protects us from our enemies. Yet, how does He protect
us from ourselves and our own sense of invincibility? When
there is a flaw within us that is not dealt with, when
there is a lifestyle of sin that goes ignored, He will allow
things to happen so that we will turn back to Him and
purge those things from our lives. Likewise, He will allow
negative things to happen to a haughty, unrepentant
church (or nation) as a whole.

AMERICA IN THE END TIME

In Ecclesiastes 3:15, we are taught God sees to it that
historical patterns repeat themselves. In fact, the Scripture reveals that to truly understand what is happening
today and to discern what will happen tomorrow, we must
be familiar with what happened yesterday. This is important because God's people in America need to know where
this nation fits into the Lord's purposes so that we will
not be taken unawares.

According to my friend Bill Cloud, there are historical
patterns unique to the 20th century that hint at what the

future might hold for this country and her citizens. Those patterns are found in the developments that led to and the consequences of both World Wars.

Few people remember, but World War I actually began as the result of an act of terror carried out by a Serb nationalist who wanted to make a political statement on behalf of his organization, the Black Hand. Unfortunately for millions of people, that statement—the murder of Frances Ferdinand, heir to the Austro-Hungarian throne, and his wife—ignited a powder keg that turned the European continent into a massive killing field.

As a consequence of that war, the balance of power in the world shifted. By the time the final shot had been fired, there was no longer a German, Austro-Hungarian, Ottoman or Russian empire. All these powers either no longer existed or, in the case of Russia, were transformed into a more sinister political entity. Consequently, with the demise of these empires came the ascent of other powers—Great Britain, France, Italy and Japan.

So, in the case of World War I, we learn that what started as an act of terror caused the powers of the earth to be shaken. Now consider the developments that led to World War II. For the United States, it began with a surprise attack from the air upon our armed and naval forces in Hawaii. But for the rest of the world, World War II began in September 1939, when Hitler invaded Poland. Yet, let us go back a bit further to September 1938.

As we mentioned, this is when Hitler threatened war unless he was given a piece of land in Czechoslovakia. He was given the land in exchange for peace. This conciliatory posture on behalf of the West simply fed his aggression, which culminated with the invasion of Poland a year later. So, I could argue that World War II started with a "land-for-peace" deal gone wrong, and for America was topped off by a surprise air attack. Can you see the picture?

The outcome of World War II was similar to the end of World War I – the balance of power shifted. Nazi Germany was destroyed and the nation split into two portions. Japan no longer had an empire and was, in fact, an occupied nation. Great Britain, though victorious, now had to take a back seat to her younger contemporary, the United States. The rise of America's power was offset by the rise of another deadly opponent, the Soviet Union. Once again we see that World War shakes the powers of the earth.

I bring this out because if the war on terror does evolve into something more—World War III perhaps—and the patterns of history hold true, then the United States, currently the world's sole superpower may devolve into a second tier nation, leaving a power vacuum across the world and setting the stage for the last end time prophecies to come to pass.

Consider again Ezekiel 38 & 39, which describes the invasion of Israel by Gog of Magog. There is no mention of help coming from anywhere except from heaven. This certainly insinuates that when this happens, either the United States is unwilling or unable to come to Israel's aid. Clearly, something happens to change the status of America between now and then. And if this does happen, American Christians should not lose heart but know that the day of our redemption is ever closer (Luke 21:28).

Most Americans think that in the continuing war on terror, we will ultimately prevail, even though we may incur casualties. But what if the war turns out to be more difficult than anyone has anticipated? The war on terror may very well lead the world into the fulfillment of some of the greatest prophecies in the Bible and if that is the case, this war will tax us in every way imaginable. In the end, our superpower status may be diminished but it has to be this way because the path will be paved for the coming Islamic beast. So, what can we do?

ESCAPING THE COMING DARKNESS

Behold now, this city is near to flee unto, and it is a little one: Oh, let me escape thither, (is it not a little one?) and my soul shall live (Genesis 19:20).

Then let them which are in Judaea flee to the mountains; and let them which are in the midst of it depart out; and let not them that are in the countries enter thereinto (Luke 21:21).

The year was 66 A.D. The Romans had surrounded the city of Jerusalem. The leader of the army was called back to Rome and, for a brief period, the city was not open. A group of Jewish rebels had decided to create an insurrection against the Roman army. They believed God would help them liberate the city from Roman occupation. Another group chose not to fight in the soon-to-be battle for Jerusalem. Instead, they fled out of the city under the criticism of the rebels. They found themselves on the other side of the Jordan River in a community called Pella.

A few years later (70 A.D.), the Roman 10th Legion returned, slaughtering the rebels, burning the temple to the ground and taking massive numbers of Jews captive. Those who escaped were Christians who remembered the words of Jesus, "When ye shall see the abomination of desolation . . . standing where it ought not, (let him that readeth understand,) . . . flee to the mountains" (Mark 13:14).

Centuries earlier, a famous prophet had sounded a warning to Israel. He revealed that the Babylonians would one day invade the holy city, destroy it and take the Hebrews captive for 70 years (Jeremiah 25:11). The fatal day came when King Nebuchadnezar and his legions roared through Judea and into Jerusalem, resulting in the first siege of the city since the time of David.

While massive numbers of Jews were forcibly marched into captivity in Babylon, a handful of God's people remained in the land, including the very prophet who pronounced the coming invasion. The prophet Jeremiah purchased property near Bethlehem, burying a title deed as a sign that God would one day bring the Jews back to their homeland.

In both instances, people escaped the danger and the captivity. One group did so by changing where they were living before the war began, and the other by a supernatural intervention of God.

AMERICA, THE LAND OF REFUGE

America is called the land of the free and the home of the brave. It could very well be nicknamed "the land of refuge." For centuries people from every nationality and socio-economic background have managed to escape countries where oppression and dictators have choked off the freedom of the masses. They have fled to America, the land of refuge.

Few people living on earth today, if given the opportunity, would not immediately pack their belongings and head to the shores of America. Throughout world history, God has always had a place of refuge for His people. In the days of the patriarchs, the Jews went to Egypt during a famine and Joseph re-located the entire clan and gave them refuge there. They lived there for 400 years, until finally returning to Israel under Moses, a nation about 2 million strong.

Noah built an ark that provided protection for his family from a global flood. Lot was told to escape to a small city called Zoar to be hidden from the destruction of Sodom and Gomorrah. Christ was carried to Egypt as an infant to escape the bloody hands of a jealous king named Herod who was bent on killing the future King of the Jews. Paul escaped a series of assassination attempts in Damascus by traveling into Arabia where he spent three years in prayer.

During the 7-year Tribulation, God will prepare a special place for a chosen Jewish remnant where they will be fed and protected from the assault of Satan and the Antichrist. The location will likely be the city of Petra, carved out of the stone mountains in the land of Edom and Moab. There is a principle in Scripture that God can provide a way of escape for the righteous if they will follow His direction.

America has been a safe haven for several centuries. We are now aware that times have changed forever. This new war is only beginning and will not end until Christ visibly returns to earth to rule for 1,000 years.

Conclusion

WHAT REALLY MATTERS MOST

The picture will be forever etched in the minds of those who witnessed it. The black smoke began pouring from the gaping holes in the Twin Towers. Billowing flames of fire began leaping from the windows, like ocean waves in a hurricane, feeding off of the jet fuel that filled the building. Suddenly, hundreds of faces appeared where windows once framed the towers. People from all ethnic groups, economic classes and religious beliefs began frantically waving for help, knowing all the time that it was impossible for firefighters to extend ladders to reach them.

The seconds seemed like minutes as the searing fire burned walls and began melting metal and vaporizing papers, wood and carpet. Only the Almighty knows the prayers and the weeping and wailing that competed with the roaring sound of the fire. As the heat and fire began burning the flesh and clothes off of innocent victims and thousands of people stood stunned at ground zero, suddenly we saw people leaping from the towers to sudden death at the feet of those on the ground. At that moment, time stopped and clashed with eternity!

One thing is certain: those who chose to jump to their deaths that day would have willingly given up their stocks, bonds, bank accounts, cars and all earthly possessions if someone could have guaranteed them an extended life with their families. At that critical moment of decision, all the hard work, long hours, overtime and education meant nothing. The reality that life can end unexpectedly, and there is nothing one can really do about it crossed the mind of every American that day!

This brings me to an important point. When the appointed time for your departure from this life comes and your soul is preparing to make its journey to either heaven or hell—to its eternal destination—what will matter most is not your wealth, your education or your prestige. The only thing that will matter will be your faith in and relationship with God, the love of your family, and the fellowship of your Christian friends.

Certainly the Bible predicts troubling times in the future. Stress will become so great that men's hearts will fail them for fear of looking after those things which are coming to pass upon the earth (see Luke 21:26). Yet, if we have a true experience with Christ and the assurance of His gift of eternal life, then death is not a threat for us. Instead, it is the door to our eternal destiny.

On September 11, 2001, millions of Americans experienced a fear that they had never encountered before. Yet, millions of Christians sensed a strong inner peace that could not be explained. Believers recognize that all things in this life are temporal and nothing will last forever, but the kingdom of God will endure for ages without end. What really counts is a personal, "born again" relationship with

God through the Lord Jesus Christ. It was God's eternal plan to send His Son, Jesus Christ, to take the sins of mankind to the cross and die in our place. Christ then arose from the dead and was seen by hundreds after His resurrection.

The proof that Jesus lives today is in His ability to transform and change the lives of those who trust in Him.

My friend, the gospel of Jesus Christ will be preached in all the world as a testimony to all nations and then the end will come (Matthew 24:14). This book is only a portion of a message to give you a warning and encourage you to receive and follow Jesus Christ.

When the final empire of man comes to an end, the earthly kingdom of Christ will be just beginning! In that moment, the kingdom of the Beast will be seized and overthrown by the Lion of the Tribe of Judah, Jesus Christ!

> And I saw heaven opened, and behold a white horse; and he that sat upon him was called Faithful and True, and in righteousness he doth judge and make war. His eyes were as a flame of fire, and on his head were many crowns; and he had a name written, that no man knew, but he himself. And he was clothed with a vesture dipped in blood: and his name is called The Word of God. And the armies which were in heaven followed him upon white horses, clothed in fine linen, white and clean. And out of his mouth goeth a sharp sword, that with it he should smite the nations: and he shall rule them with a rod of iron: and he treadeth the winepress of the fierceness and wrath of Almighty God. And he hath on his vesture and on his thigh a name written, KING OF KINGS, AND LORD OF LORDS (Revelaion 19:11-16).

The Priceless Page

Have you been born again?

Have you accepted Jesus Christ as your personal Savior and Lord?

If you have been out of fellowship with God, or have never experienced a personal relationship with Christ, then pray this prayer aloud—from your heart:

Dear Jesus, I believe you are the Son of God. I believe that you died for my sins and that you were buried and rose again from the dead. I believe that today, you are seated in heaven with the Heavenly Father and you are hearing my prayer.

Lord Jesus, forgive me of my sins. Cleanse my spirit and mind by your precious blood. I repent and turn away from my sins and from my past, and I will begin a new life today as your child! I receive Christ as my Savior. Thank you, Lord. Amen.

If you have accepted Christ, then write to us and let us know. In order to effectively follow Christ, you must learn more of God's Word and spend time with other believers who can help you grow. There are many good churches and pastors who can help teach you the Word of God and nurture you in the Lord.

If we do not meet in this life, then by the Grace of God, we will meet in heaven.

– Evangelist Perry Stone

BIBLIOGRAPHY

Abigail Radoszkowicz "For Allah's Sake" in *The Jerusalem Post*, February 20, 2001.

Alexander Roberts, James Donaldson, Henry Wace, Editors. *Early Church Fathers: Ante-Nicene Fathers*, Volumes 4, 5. (Peabody, MA: Hendrickson, 1995).

Alexander Stille, "Radical New Views of Islam and the Origins of the Koran" *The New York Times*, March 2, 2002.

Avi Ben Mordechai. *Signs in the Heavens* (Woodland Park, CO: Millenium 7,000, 1997).

Alexander Nemets, "Expert: Russia Knew in Advance, Encouraged Citizens to Cash Out Dollars" *http:www.newsmax.com/archives/articles.shtml*.

Bagila Bukharbayeva, "Magic lamb comforts Uzbek Muslims" *The Nando Times*, June 27, 2002.

Flavius Josephus, *The Works of Josephus* (Peabody, MA: Hendrickson, 1998).

Geoffrey W. Bromily, William Sanford LaSor, Edgar W. Smith, Everett F. Harrison, Roland K. Harrison, Eds. *International Standard Bible Encyclopedia* (Grand Rapids: Eerdmans, 1994).

Hal Lindsey, *The Final Battle* (Palos Verdes, CA: Western Front, 1995).

http://www.freeyellow.com/members5/unitedstatesofislam/index.html.

http://www.spacedaily.com.

http://www.users.dircon.co.uk/!netking/murabitn.htm.

"How Israel gave Away Judaism's Most Sacred Site" in *Moment*, June 2002.

Howard Blum, *The Gold of Exodus* (New York: Simon & Schuster, 1998).

Immanuel Velokovsky. *Ages In Chaos* (Garden City, NY: Country Live, 1952).

"Islam Tightens Its Grip on Jerusalem" in *Israel Today*, December 2001.

J. M. Rodwell, Tr. *The Koran* (New York: Ballantine Books, 1993).

Joseph Telushkin, *Jewish Literacy: The Most Important Things to Know About the Jewish Religion, Its People and Its History* (New York: William Morrow, 1991).

Luis Bush, "What is the 10-40 Window?" *http:www.worldnet daily.com/ news.asp?ARTICLE_ID=24755*

Manuel Komroff, Ed. *The Travels of Marco Polo* (New York: Modern Library, 1926).

Matthew Fordahl, "Sun, Six Planets To Line Up" *Washington Post*, April 5, 2000.

Notes from a personal interview in Jerusalem, November 30, 2001.

Dr. Peter Michas. *The Spiritual Birth Date of Messiah Yeshua* (Troy IL: Messengers of the Messiah, 1998).

Randolph E. Schmid, "Snake with Legs Fossil Found" *http:www.2think.org/ snakelegs.shtml.*

Reuters News Service, July 11, 2001

Roy A. Reinhold, "Other Scholarship Proving the Exact Date of Birth of Yeshua (Jesus)" *http://hometown.aol.com/prophecy04/ index.html.*

Shahabuddin, "The Coming of Mystery Imam al-Mahdi" *The Sunday Times*, November 18, 1990.

Tatyana Koryagina, "The Dollar and America Will Fall Down on August 19" *Pravda*, July 8, 2001.

The New York Times, International Edition, October 11, 1990.

"The Riddle of the Dome of the Rock," *Internet Newsletter* July 29, 2001. *www.templemountfaithful.org.*

Time, September 18, 2001.

Victor Paul Wierwille. *Jesus Christ, Our Promised Seed* (New Knoxville OH: American Christian, 1982).

Voice of the Martyrs magazine, P.O. Box 443, Bartlesville, OK.

Wall Street Journal, November 1, 2002.

W. E. Vine , Merrill F. Unger, Willam White, Ed. *Vine's Expository Dictionary of Old and New Testament Words.* (Nashville, Tennessee: Thomas Nelson) 1996.

"Who Is Imam Mahdi?" http://*www.naqshbandi.net/haqqani/qiyama/ imam.html*

William Whiston, Tr. *Josephus Complete Works* (Grand Rapids: Kregel, 1960).